HADASSAH MULOWA K. KAJOBA

Shattered Masterpiece

The End Matters Finish Strong

PLATYPUS
PUBLISHING

First published by Platypus Publishing 2024

Copyright © 2024 by Hadassah Mulowa K. Kajoba

All rights reserved. No part of this publication may be reproduced, stored or transmitted in any form or by any means, electronic, mechanical, photocopying, recording, scanning, or otherwise without written permission from the publisher. It is illegal to copy this book, post it to a website, or distribute it by any other means without permission.

Hadassah Mulowa K. Kajoba asserts the moral right to be identified as the author of this work.

First edition

ISBN: 978-1-962133-39-5

DEDICATION

To my parents, good people with golden hearts. They shared the best of themselves with the world and advised me: 'To only fear God and respect everyone else.' I dance with gratitude throughout my life's journey to the melody of these words. To those I love! They fuel my life in countless ways and there is no Me without Them. My daughter, thank you for inspiring ideas for this book seven years ago. Back then, I was not ready.

Now, it is ready to go to souls with untold stories and unsung melodies. Remember, you've got this!

WHAT THEY SAID

"Mira's story teaches us the power of determination, persistence, and picking oneself up despite the challenges encountered. It calls us to keep moving forward even in the face of struggles and finding strength in faith and a support system."

Sandra F.

"Mira's stories of resilience will inspire those who have experienced frustration, betrayal or made impulsive decisions to persevere. Her stories also show the cost of pursuing dreams and the reward of never giving up. Mira reminds us that there is a will, there is always a way. The secret is to persevere as the storms run their course."

DD.

HADASSAH SAYS

"Everything considered, I am just a speck that God gave weight to. So, in this suspended billions-year-old universe, a strong wind can blow me away in a fraction of a second, and my story will be history as fast. To be meaningful, I learned to give, grow, and love."

Contents

DEDICATION iii
WHAT THEY SAID v
HADASSAH SAYS vi
INTRODUCTION 2
PART 1: HER UPBRINGING 4
   Story 1: Her Childhood World 5
   Story 2: Beacons of Hope and Guiding Lights 10
   Story 3: From Dusty Recesses to Fallen Hope 14
   Story 4: Rising Strength 19
PART 2: MIRA LEAVES FOR SCHOOL 29
   Story 5: Welcome to Switzerland 30
   Story 6: Life's Sense of Humor 33
PART 3: A NEW DOOR OPENS 40
   Story 7: Bound By Faith Farewell 41
   Story 8: Cultural Contrasts & New Beginnings 46
   Story 9: Dream-chase and A Warm Surprise 50
PART 4: IN THE EYE OF THE STORM 55
   Story 10: Unforeseen Welcomes 56
   Story 11: Taking a Stand 66
   Story 12: The Unforeseen 75
Part 5: MIRA KEPT MOVING 83
   Story 13-The Shift 84
   Story 14: The Time Came 91

Story 15: Journey to the Past 102
PART 6: MIRA FACES MIRA 114
Story 16: The Ironic Poetry 115
Story 17: Rising Through Brokenness 125
Story 18: Embracing the Inner Warrior 133
CONCLUSION 141
HEAL & BLOOM 144
Introduction 146
Definitions 148
Key Lessons 149
Practical Food for Thought 153
Summary 156
....157
ACKNOWLEDGEMENT 158
ABOUT THE AUTHOR 161

INTRODUCTION

> "Jump off the passenger seat and take the wheel to direct your life toward your better self." *Kajoba, H. M. K., 2023.*

Have you ever felt the sting of life's harsh slap, leaving you yearning for balance? Yes? Meet Mira and join her on an extraordinary journey as she defies the odds stacked against her.

Born and raised in Africa, the time came; she packed light, took leaps of faith, and left the familiar to become a better version of herself in foreign lands. Unprepared, this journey led through endless storms. Upon finally finding stable ground, it crumbled beneath her, leaving her on sinking sand, prompting her to question her worth. Exhausted and overwhelmed by life, she realized it was time to stop drifting with the current; she was the current itself. There are chapters she wished to erase from her memory. Yet, Mira embraced her depths, discovered that periods of stagnation and turbulence are integral to life, and refused to allow circumstances to impede her flow. She confronted obstacles intended to break her, rose from setbacks, and was determined to pursue her dreams and aspirations. In the end, she understood the gains are infinite when we make our lives meaningful.

So, Dear Masterpiece, whatever the reason you picked up this book, I am glad you are here to travel alongside Mira on her quest for becoming. Will she find solace in the company of strangers? Or will the cost of her quest prove too high? May her short stories inspire you to embrace your unique path forward, confront challenges head-on, and finish strong. During defining moments, remember the journey also matters.

The book concludes with 'Heal and Bloom: A Life Simple Self-Help Tool to Thrive,' offering guidance on self-agency.

Let us dive into the book. PART 1: HER UPBRINGING gives you a glimpse into this little girl's life. Watch her grow right in your eyes! Across the eighteen stories, discover the depths of Mira's resilience and the transformative power of self-agency.

PART 1: HER UPBRINGING

Welcome to Mira's captivating journey, which embodies the saying, "A tree cannot stand without roots." In Part 1, you will find the following three stories:

- Story 1: Her Childhood World
- Story 2: Beacons of Hope and Guiding Lights
- Story 3: From Dusty Recesses to Fallen Hope

Story 1: Her Childhood World

Childhood Adventures

Mira grew up in a closed community in Zaire, Africa, where they believed in the saying: it takes a village to raise a child. A person could walk the longest stretch in an hour.

The children played unconcerned about safety, and their joyful voices filled the air. So, it was easy to predict when they fought because silence would betray them. They often resolved the issues, with watchful adults stepping in as necessary. Children even took advantage of unforeseen events. Sometimes, the water motor pump would break, taking a while to fix. So, families would gather by the riverside to do laundry and fetch water. Children turned this event into an amusement park. They ran back and forth, splashing water, competing to hold their breath underwater for the longest, and much more.

When it was time to leave, they helped gather clothes drying on the grass. Mira gathered pebbles and shells to play with her sister Delia, who was born with a physical disability and did not walk.

The community thrived as well. Parents prayed together, taking turns hosting the event and sharing light refreshments. There were more events throughout the year, such as Christmas, New Year, and Easter. While in session, school performances and community services reinforced a sense of home.

Of all the celebrations, Christmas was her favorite. It was outdoors in Mira's backyard; young boys and girls would set up benches from the Church and tables from school to share meals. When it rained, the festivities continued in their respective homes. Some of Mira's favorite moments included a cherished home tradition of competing to determine who would cook the most delicious meal or bake the most exquisite cake.

Mira loved these special events. She received new outfits from her parents or passed down from her older sisters. Wearing their clothes was not just a fashion choice but a source of immense pride as their attire carried a piece of her sisters' personalities, connecting her to their strength and intelligence. Besides hand-me-downs, her mother gave her a sewing machine and would buy her fabrics. Allowing her creativity to run wild, she made dresses, skirts, or pants and sometimes imitated her sister's outfits. With the remnant pieces of clothes, she made dolls and their dresses to play with Delia. Mira's childhood was a mosaic of shared joy and connection.

Backyard and Nature Delights

Now, imagine a backyard with wild mushrooms growing during the rainy season. Mira's favorite was Terya in her native language or Tintin by everyone else. They emerged from the ground like small balls, then unfolded into a glossy brown and white color, releasing an earthy, breath-taking beauty. Tintin could grow large enough to hide an antelope during heavy rains. It was a legend Mira hoped to witness one day. There were other types of mushrooms, red, yellow, and white shades, making her backyard a great delight, and Mira's mom allowed her to cook the one she picked. It sparked her lifelong love for mushrooms. Someone once said: "a fly without guidance follows the corpse to the grave." There were also poisonous mushrooms, but Mira stuck to the familiar ones to avoid taking unnecessary and deadly risks.

Nature offered more delights! The community's edge was a stunning chain of small mountains. For leisure, youth groups would arrange hikes on the mountaintops, where a colossal cross constructed from barrels stood tall, visible from great distances. This landmark also captivated countless visitors; some would climb to touch it. The hikes offered an aerial view of the community, and Mira's imagination grew wings. She would close her eyes and let the wind take her away toward a destiny filled with greatness. She stood on the mountaintop feeling invincible and fired up to tackle the world. All she wanted was to serve the greater good.

There was one thing unsettling, the local cemetery, which was visible from her front yard. Little did she know it would become a haunting reminder of lost opportunities and a profound part of her journey.

How was it at home?

Familial Curfews and Bonding

Mira grew up with no watch. She did not need it; the rule at home was to return before sunset, or the chickens returned to their coop between 5 and 5:30 pm. Breaking the curfew was playing with fire, and the most severe punishment was losing playtime—it may be more painful than depriving a child of their cell phone or video games today. Children could stay past curfew if parents agreed and there was no homework, upcoming quizzes, or exams. Once home, bedtime was 8:00 pm every day, except Fridays and Saturdays. During the weekends, everyone looked forward to watching TV or movies after school or finishing chores unless there was a school play, which became the night's highlight. The family would also gather for singing, praying, and storytelling, and Mira's parents would share their life wisdom with everyone. If someone did something wrong, the gathering would become a teachable moment, making it awkward for the guilty party. These corrective measures were necessary to suppress any misconduct before it could escalate.

Mira differed from the girls at home. As a tomboy and proud to defy traditional gender norms, she hunted with boys, joined them in butchering, and helped with car repairs. As a reward, her mother exempted her from kitchen duties, which upset some girls in the house, yet they would not join the guys. Then, Mira's mom removed the gender divide and asked everyone to take turns in the kitchen. The girls celebrated this shift more than the boys did. Over time, it became natural for everyone and even enjoyable.

Her mom established kitchen rules to reduce food waste and ensure everyone had enough to eat. If someone cooked too little, they would leave the table sooner. If someone cooked too much, they would have to stay and finish the leftovers. Not only did people become responsible, but the rule strengthened familial bonds as coalitions formed to help each other empty plates. In the end, everyone learned how to cook. Mira's home was a sanctuary for anyone who needed food, shelter, and much more.

Her parents created a home embodying the genuine sense of an open-door policy. Mira wanted to be like them one day.

Who were Mira's parents?

Story 2: Beacons of Hope and Guiding Lights

Mira's Mom–A Rare Soul

Can you imagine a teen having to drop out of high school to get married as the best option? That was Mira's mom!

Tuition was expensive. She dropped out of school and got married. It was a better choice instead of settling for life's crumbs that illiteracy would offer. It broke her heart to quit school. After marrying the love of her life, with the full support of her husband, this brilliant young girl, now a mother, trained to be a midwife. She started working at the local clinic, catering to neighboring villages and assisting countless mothers in delivering their babies. Mira recalled the distressing knocks on their front door late at night, and her mother would rush to the clinic to help mothers in labor, regardless of the time or weather. She also self-taught various technical skills, including sewing, knitting, cooking, baking, and much more. After years of working as a midwife, she changed the first career to use her new skills teaching pastors' wives at a local women's school so they could further support their households. Her drive for personal growth led her to become the school's director. She continued to serve with compassion, helping countless women and their families.

As time passed, she left the school to venture on her own. Her business thrived, and the future was bright. Looking back, in the rhythmic cadence of her daily life, she assumed the role of orchestrator, ensuring harmony and joy within her home and beyond. Her maternal love radiated warmth in countless souls, including students and strangers. The broader influence of her passion to serve attested to the power of rising from humble beginnings and remaining selfless. She was a timeless reminder that goodness never goes out of style, and Mira felt honored to call her 'Ma.' More about her remarkable soul unfolds in **Story 13**.

A Man with a Mind Made Up

Mira's dad sold vegetables in the local faith-based community as a young boy to earn money and help his father, a land cultivator. He wanted to enroll in school, but the diverging doctrines between the church his parents attended and the one where he traded goods prevented it. So, he admired the renowned schools from a distance. Unlike Mira's mother, poverty did not impede his formal education. His parents could afford his tuition.

One day, a foreign missionary noticed his intelligence and hard work. He offered to help him enroll in school. His dad (Mira's grandpa) accepted without hesitation. Mira's dad took the blessing and ran with it. Equipped with a drive for knowledge, he broke societal norms that kept children in villages trapped in cycles of illiteracy and its resulting consequences.

While in high school, he met Mira's mother and they got married. Then, he, his wife, and children went to Europe where he got a Doctorate degree in theology. He returned to work in his community, being among the few black individuals in the country with that degree. Mira's father taught the Old Testament and Hebrew at the local university and served as a pastor.

Later in his profession, he became the first black dean of the university and earned the Emeritus title. To Mira, he was the most accomplished and humble man she knew. He believed in self-sufficiency and personal development. While the world revered this visionary mastermind, to Mira, he was just 'Dad.' We will share more about him in **Part 5**. His remarkable work and life ethics inspired hope.

An Inspiring Glance

Mira's parents were her role models. As a movement, they devoted their lives to inspiring countless people, and their union lasted for almost four decades, sharing the best of themselves with the world. She never witnessed her parents arguing while growing up. So, Mira lived her life without resorting to aggression and believed that beyond all adversities, there is a breakthrough, provided there was a willing heart, strong values, and faith in God to push through.

"If my parents, a high school dropout and a vegetable trader, could rise from little to empowering the masses, so could I," she convinced herself.

The soil where her parents' journey began is also where hers took root. She inherited a roadmap that summed up to **fear no one but God**. Equipped with such wisdom, she stepped into the world feeling unstoppable, with parents as beacons of hope and guiding lights.

Story 3: From Dusty Recesses to Fallen Hope

A Little Background

Growing up, Mira was a child like any other who loved playing. Her team was among the best during competing games, such as dancing, somersaulting, jumping rope, and more. In addition, she loved crafting clay objects and cloth dolls to play with Delia. During her teen years, she spent time hunting, butchering, and learning car repair with her brothers and cousins. She looked forward to these moments traditionally reserved for boys. Mira felt limitless.

The community was self-sufficient. There was a kindergarten, primary and secondary schools. She could even attend university there as well. The secondary school welcomed students from many places, and they lived in boarding houses, which brought more excitement to the area. Mira looked forward to the weekend. It was for community service or mountain hiking, and students loved it. In addition to Sunday Church gatherings, these were the few times students in boarding had a flexible curfew; they could hang out longer. These events fostered unity, and Mira looked forward to these days. As Mira grew older, her academic journey took a challenging turn, and she struggled with the demands of secondary school, which attacked her character and shook her to the core.

How was Mira in school?

Early Years of Character Forging

Picture young Mira in kindergarten singing and reciting poems with her classmates. Then the teachers give them delicious porridge, and warm milk with handmade cookies. After eating, they learn some more. An hour before dismissal of primary school, parents, or appointees came to pick the kids up. For Mira, it was her mother or a sibling who picked her up. Equipped with her kindergarten skill set, she entered the first grade of primary school. Mira had friends, but they moved away by fourth grade, which was heartbreaking. Moving from one class to another brought new connections and unique challenges, which tempered the blow and pain of separation. In general, she loved school, except for a few things.

Students looked forward to recess to play jump rope, tag, somersault, and many other games. But, just before the break, teachers would spring surprise quizzes. Taking too long robbed students of time from the 30 minutes of pure joy; failing meant no recess. There was an alternative to the latter-physical reprimands. They included in-class spanking, paddling, and at home writing sentences 1000 times at home. After the punishments, students joined their friends outside. For her, recess was the best time in school. So, she refused to miss it. Over the six years of primary school, even her competitive nature did not spare her from the reprimands.

Parents knew about these practices and did not mind, as they helped shape character. When teachers abused their authority, parents intervened, and students were happy to see the teachers in trouble. Her mom showed up once ready to hurt the teacher who spanked and bruised Mira on her calves, and she never got punished again. She continued enjoying recess, returning home covered in dust. Her mother did not mind, provided playing did not affect school performance.

Other than losing recess time, Mira did not like the outdoor grade sharing at selected milestones. During these events, teachers aligned students per class and called their names from the top to the lowest grades to give them their certificates. These public events put pressure on everyone in school. That is not all! Each class sang songs to praise high achievers and ridiculed low performers. Were these punitive measures effective? That was debatable. But those bullied never got the courage to return to school.

Mira was a risk taker. She would choose reprimand instead of missing recess. But failing classes was out of the question. She was unwilling to suffer the humiliating consequences. So, she chose academic excellence. Besides, it was priceless to see the smiles on her parents' faces when she brought home good grades. It fueled an addictive internal sense of accomplishment.

At the end of the year, she remained among the best students, if not the best. Mira played hard and remained dedicated to school. Armed with this mindset, she entered secondary school ready to face new challenges.

A Period Gone Wrong

Mira entered secondary school, which also took six years to complete. Everything was smooth sailing until the third year, when she had an awkward moment. One day, she raised her hand to solve a math problem. Confident to do well, she walked to the front, and what had started as simple whispers grew into mocking laughter when she reached the board.

Something was wrong. Next, her teacher walked her out of the classroom to tell her she bled through her khaki Conroe skirt. Then he collected her school bag while she waited, embarrassed and wishing she could disappear. Mira went home, covering the stain with a sweater. Her mother, ever supportive, comforted her but also warned her:

> "If you play with boys now that you can menstruate, you will get pregnant."

She found these words more embarrassing than staining her skirt and the subsequent mocking laughter.

> *"That is not how it works!"* Mira said to herself.

However, she got the message. It took her about a week to overcome the embarrassment and return to school. Students whispered and murmured after seeing her, but she remained composed, and time removed the sting of humiliation. After the incident, Mira was never the same. This harsh awakening shifted her view of life altogether understanding that people could be cruel. In her mind, she grew from a girl to a woman. Adding to the challenge, Mira faced betrayal for the first time.

Story 4: Rising Strength

The Stains of Lies and Deception

Mira, now a teenager, was exploring her romantic life. On weekends, students living in the boarding house could stay away from their dormitories longer than on weekdays. At Mira's house, the childhood rule of returning home before the chickens remained effective. One weekend, Mira, in love, took an unnecessary risk and broke the curfew. Her boyfriend and she spent time together at school later, after community service, before he returned to the boarding house. They were sitting on the edge of the school building facing the office of Mira's dad, which was next to the Church. Since there were no cell phones back then, imagine how thrilled she was to see her best friend walking by as she headed to Mira's home. They had a quick conversation before parting ways.

"Please tell my mom I am on my way," she said.

"No problem," her friend responded.

As the sun set and darkness approached, the chickens had returned to their coop, and she knew punishment awaited. Luckily, the school was just a few minutes away on foot. About fifteen minutes after speaking to her friend, Mira arrived home to find her mother angry and fuming.

"Where have you been?" she asked multiple times while reprimanding Mira.

Confused, frightened, and drenched in tears, Mira watched her friend disappear around the corner of the house.

"What did she tell Mom?" Mira wondered.

Eventually, her mother calmed down and apologized for trusting a stranger over her daughter and promised never to spank her again. While Mira's sisters de-escalated the situation, Mira wanted to know what happened. She had never seen her mother that angry and wanted answers to move on. She turned to her sisters.

"Mom asked where you were, and your friend said she did not know. But community service finished long ago. On her way here, she saw someone like you with a boy heading to the men's restrooms," her sisters told Mira.

"Why did she lie?" Mira inquired from her sisters, trying to understand.

However, no one knew; they were all left to speculate on the motive. Indeed, "what bites is often under your clothes." They were very close, so her lies stung in Mira's soul, marking the end of their friendship and introduction to betrayal.

Self-defense

Mira and her boyfriend continued dating. One day, they planned to meet just before attending Sunday service at Church. While her parents talked little about intimacy, the message was unmistakable: abstain until marriage, and Mira told her boyfriend that physical intimacy was out of the question. He respected her decision. They planned to meet for sweet talk and innocent kisses to mark the occasion, looking forward to the next time they would see each other. However, the plan for romance took a frightening shift. It became an ambush orchestrated by the boyfriend and his friends to take her innocence. She fought and escaped but could not confide in anyone. The meeting was never supposed to happen; therefore, she internalized everything at first. The next day, false rumors about her passing her cookies spread like wildfire, leaving behind traces of gossip and lies that spiked like thorns, ruining her reputation. Humiliated, ashamed, and facing the daunting task of returning to school daily in a small community, Mira found refuge at home from her brother, who helped her through it. She was the victim of a sinister plot that created an unsettling aura and marked the end of their relationship.

It was time to pick herself up from being prey, fight back, and reclaim her dignity. So, she awakened the hunter in her to face the lurking shadows of deceitfulness and devised a plan:

> *"I will date a few boys and break up with them all. They will soon discover I never slept with anyone."*

The tight-knit community played in her favor. Over time, more people vouched for the truth, So Mira's plan worked, and things got better after clearing her name. The adolescent misfortunes hurt her school performance; she repeated the third grade.

From that incident, Mira became mindful of trusting others. The next year, she passed. Mira even developed meaningful friendships. Most of her new friends were male, which aligned with her tomboy personality. It made her social circle feel natural. She was herself once again.

Next, she joined the school performance team. The play director exempted participants from some school assignments. It worked for Mira. She preferred memorizing scripts over studying for tests. Also, being on stage felt therapeutic and helped her prepare for the world, the most significant stage.

She promised herself not to take any unnecessary risks, and with her father's office across from her high school, Mira felt even safer. It was a constant reminder that he was always there to protect her. The rest was a matter of her doing the right thing, so she pledged never to sleep with anyone and to wait to marry her high school sweetheart, whoever that would be.

Two years later, she met Francois.

Mira In Love

Mira entered her final year of secondary school in love with Francois, who graduated a year before. They were in their second year of dating and planned to get married. Mira's mother knew about their intention and accepted Francois as a future son-in-law, seeing how much her daughter loved him. One thing stood in their way, the national three-day State Exam, to finish school. Then she would enroll at the university, and they would get married. The test required extensive study to pass since it was comprehensive. To study, students looked for quiet areas. During this time, those in the boarding house had permission to be away but stay in the school's vicinity. So many students isolated themselves in the nearby bushes.

Do you remember the ambush from a few years ago?

Mira wanted a safe and quiet place to prepare for the exam. Uncomfortable being alone in the bush, she chose a house under construction near her home. She spread her African wrap on the ground and dive into her notebooks. One day, when she went to her usual spot, some high school boys had climbed into the building frame and startled her while two more hiding in the other rooms joined. Frightened, she fought off the one who grabbed her first and escaped in time. If there were doors, the situation could have been much worse. Out of breath and frightened, she confided in someone and could not wait to tell her soon-to-be fiancé, Francois, who planned to visit her that weekend. Relieved to have his support, Mira trusted he would handle the situation and did not care to know how he'd do it.

During his visit, Mira told him everything; he was angry and promised to address it, and she stood tall, feeling invincible and vindicated. The next day, they sat under their favorite tree in Mira's front yard when Francois' demeanor changed. Mira sensed a gloomy atmosphere but did not know what was happening. When she asked Francois about it, he responded with disgust and disdain, leaving her hurt and disappointed.

"You lied to me. What you told me is not what happened," Francois said, tears streaming down his face.

"Why would the person who told me what you did lie? I respected your wishes and waited for you, but you were intimate with other people." He continued.

His words flew like spikes of glasses landing on her heart. Looking into Francois's eyes, there was nothing Mira could say. She cried, reminiscing about the attempted assault, including the one three years earlier. The memory compounded the agony of her relationship's death as she sat on the grass with her back turned against the front porch and facing the cemetery that had once scared her. There was nothing she could do. He was gone.

"Why won't he believe me? They could have hurt me!"

She sobbed, her internal thoughts echoing more pain and feeling abandoned. However, nothing pierced her heart the most, as François did not trust her during these vulnerable times. Later, Mira walked with him to hitchhike a ride back to his town. Crashed by their breakup, their silence echoed more pain, and her heart sank deeper. They ran into Mira's father, who was returning from the cornfield. Unaware of the split, he spoke to Francois and addressed him as "son," a term he had never used.

"Au revoir, papa." He responded.

Their brief exchange was a poignant reminder of their bitter goodbye, marking the last chapter of their romance with her father accepting Francois as his son. A car stopped to offer him a ride; he leaned in to kiss her on the cheek and walked away without looking back.

Not sure why and how, but Mira felt responsible for the breakup even though she was the victim.

Stubborn Determination

She had her romantic life all planned: Become engaged, married, have children, two girls and two boys - and serve the greater good. Unfortunately, she trusted the wrong person and his lies sniffed the life out of her hope of becoming a wife. Mira had met Francois's mother and she welcomed her with warmth. She spoke to his brother who lived in Europe. They even discussed dowry. So, for Mira, marriage was eminent. All of it was now behind her.

Despite being heartbroken and unable to concentrate on her studies, she still took the exam with a scattered mind and failed. The results announcement was public nationwide. Two people in the house took the exam. So, it was difficult to celebrate her cousin's success while mourning her own failure. Her intelligence was a significant part of her persona, and the failure wounded her reputation, leaving her with no place to hide. However, she put aside the shame of studying with peers who had caught up with her and retook the test. This time, she passed the State Exam.

Looking back, she had lost two years of repeating classes in high school, and both times involved attempted sexual assaults and lies. Mira also dreamed of marrying her high school sweetheart like her parents, but that dream fell apart. Later, she understood people will use any means when determined to hurt and ruin you.

Left with two options: stay down or pick herself up, she chose the latter. Francois learned the truth from one boy who startled Mira and wanted to reconcile, but Mira had already learned to live without him. She could have confronted the one person she confided in after the incident but rose above it and matured through the pain.

Her eyes set on furthering her education and with a renewed sense of purpose, Mira left behind the scars of the past and focused on a future filled with possibilities. She looked forward to her university dream to unfold. In the meantime, her mother inspired her to start her own business trading goods. She earned enough to cover her basic needs, and her parents provided the rest.

Knock, knock!

An African proverb said, "The arrow of time is unstoppable; it flies ever forward." Mira looked back; it had been two more years since graduating high school. Adding to that, the repeated classes totaled four years lost. She wanted to have a fiancé, be at the university, or both, but had neither and felt unaccomplished.

> "Look at you, still alone and stuck. Had you made it work with Francois, you would have been at least a wife by now."

As self-doubt flooded her mind, she felt lost. However, Mira had this unique ability to refocus her thoughts, so she reminded herself that furthering her education and becoming a wife and mother was not a matter of if, but when. Just like that, she moved on. Attending university in her home country of Zaire was out of the question. The hazing rituals were too harsh and scary. Mira was not going to be part of it. So, her dream was to study abroad, where a diploma held more value. Her father had done it before; she could do it too. God would reveal the path to her extraordinary destiny with time.

The time came, and God answered her prayer. Her older sister and brother-in-law living in Europe invited her to join them. Eager and excited, young adult Mira set off for a big adventure, leaving everything behind and heading to a land far, far away. She carried a small suitcase, tons of invaluable lessons from her childhood and teenage years, and the wisdom gained at home, founded on always keeping **God at the forefront**. She was ready to further her education.

PART 2: MIRA LEAVES FOR SCHOOL

- Story 5: Welcome to Switzerland
- Story 6: Life's Sense of Humor

Story 5: Welcome to Switzerland

Bittersweet Dream Chase

The weight of the lost time was off her shoulders. Filled with anticipation, Mira was on her way to further her education. It took months to get her visa, and the wait planted seeds of insecurity and uncertainty. But she was not alone. Her brother and other family members saw her through this vulnerability and encouraged her to be patient.

Then, the Embassy called. Within a week of the call, she was ready to join her sister, brother-in-law, nephew, and niece in Europe. On the way to the airport, she reminisced about the familiar landscape as the wind squeezed through the cracked open windows, whispering melancholic goodbyes. Tears welled up as she stared at her passport, not expecting cutting the umbilical cord to enter a new life phase would be overwhelming. She then took a deep breath, closed her eyes, and whispered to the wind.

"Now is the time to expand."

The cocoon had weathered all the weather, and the butterfly was ready to emerge. So, Mira boarded the plane, committed to growing and exploring new horizons. As they ascended thousands of feet, the flight attendant placed a meal tray before her.

The aroma of the spices wafting from the plate signaled an upcoming enriching cultural experience.

Living the Dream

The plane landed, and Mira was excited to step onto solid ground. After clearing the customs, she bought Swiss chocolate and headed to the train station. Speaking French helped her navigate the airport and catch the train on time. As it moved along, the view outside was breathtaking, with majestic mountains and vast landscapes stretching as far as the eye could see. The sheer magnificence of the landscape added a sense of awe and wonder to her journey. About three hours later, Mira's brother-in-law picked her up. History surrounded her as they drove through the town; some buildings held untold stories, while others whispered tales of the past.

Uniting with her sister, niece, and nephew, Mira felt at home and grateful for the warm welcome and the chance to bond with family. It was time to go to sleep. Mira soaked everything in, placing her clothes in the enormous closet. From her room, Mira could access the attic, but was hesitant. She watched too many scary movies, and attics held dark secrets, but it piqued her curiosity so much that she could not resist. It was a whole other room in her room, but nothing eventful. She could also see the city lights below from her third-floor bedroom and knew her future was bright. Then, she jumped into her queen-sized bed - a long-awaited dream - and slept like a log, confident of a great tomorrow.

Furthering education was no longer a distant dream but an attainable reality, as she was in the right place at the right time. Mira was ready. They headed to the first school but hit a roadblock. Mira's brother-in-law needed to be a citizen, but it was not a big deal. From the list they compiled for her, there were more schools to visit. So, Mira caught the train to see a few more and came home with a made-up mind. They scheduled an appointment, and she was looking forward to it!

Story 6: Life's Sense of Humor

A Painful Offer

One day, her brother-in-law and sister called her to join them in the living room. When she walked in, she saw nothing celebratory. Mira knew something was wrong and approached with apprehension.

> "I'm afraid there's been a change in the plan. I have accepted a new job offer, which is a fantastic opportunity." Her brother-in-law struggled to convey the news.

After congratulating him, Mira could not fathom why he seemed sad. Then her sister delivered the heartbreaking news. They had to move out of the country. She switched to Swahili in seconds, explaining that her little sister needed to return home until they settled down, and asked her to keep hope alive.

Reality sank in, and so did her heart. She grappled with conflicting emotions, celebrating her brother-in-law and mourning her fate. It felt like in high school when she faced celebrating her cousin passing the State Exam but mourned her failure. It was devastating. She excused herself and retreated to her bedroom to put God on trial.

> "Why, God, why bring me here only to send me back? I celebrate my brother-in-law's promotion, but why crush my dream in that blessing? How much more of my life must I waste doing

nothing? If You knew the trip was not your plan for me, why grant it in the first place?"

With each unanswered question, Mira felt lost, and the deepening disappointment engulfed her in an indescribable internal rage. Someone once said: "Sometimes, the night is so deep that even the bravest stars lose their way." The burden of her crashed academic hope cast dark shadows over her spirit. Past pains resurfaced, and they deepened the roots of insecurity. Mira needed an escape, but the weight of the news was crippling.

A voice whispered: *"Stop dreaming. You will never amount to anything."*

Her weeping blurred the following steps as she continued yelling in silence and wrestling with the humbling paradox of having everything and nothing at the same time. She hoped to return one day to her community as a professional, not unaccomplished. Such success would have erased the lingering memory of past pains. Mira was angry with God and accused Him of injustice for misleading her, and she was tired of having to be strong. The star within her was losing its sparks in mourning the unmet academic expectations. She grew bitter, and the emotional turmoil felt like a slow and painful death.

As her world fell apart, she still needed to help her sister- and brother-in-law pack. After they left, the longer she waited to catch the flight back to Zaire, the more the house felt like a prison with walls echoing her misfortunes. Desperately longing for the nightmare to end, returning home became the escape she needed to restore internal peace.

With this mindset, she summoned the strength to process the disappointments recorded by her pillow and was ready to leave Switzerland behind and head toward the unknown.

The Reverse Irony and A Strange Hope

The day came to catch the flight back to Africa. Do you remember where her brother-in-law picked her up a few months earlier?

Mira returned to that train station and caught the train to the airport. During the ride, she contemplated the same majestic mountains. Instead of welcoming her, they waved goodbye. Two and a half hours later, she handed over her one-way airplane ticket, buckled her seat, and the plane took off. As it gained altitude, Mira's dream seemed to dissipate, but she pledged not to shed tears even though the internal tug-of-war between happy and sad tilted the emotional scale toward crying.

She gathered and repackaged the pieces of her vision, reminding herself to take nothing for granted. Hours later, the plane landed in France for a connecting flight to Zambia. Exploring the airport and treating herself to some chocolate, much like she did in Switzerland, was uneventful. She wanted the trip to her homeland to be over. It was time to catch the next flight. The once enjoyable meal became unappetizing. To avoid spiraling into the land of negative thoughts, she slept, and it worked! In no time, the airplane landed in Zambia.

An African proverb states, "it is easier to tame a wild dog in the village than to control a mad dog in town."

Mira had faced adversities in the past, and dealing with people in a close community was manageable. But her shattered dream of furthering her education was based on hope, thus abstract, and bruised her soul. Therefore, returning to a place she hoped to escape revived forgotten pains and disappointments. However, God, in His faithfulness, helped her realize the only path forward was to retreat. Looking back, a strange spring of hope removed the sting of the failed attempts to study in Switzerland. Let us go on a soulful journey to understand it!

A Strange Well of Hope

Growing up in Africa, the community held impactful prayer sessions each week, and Mira participated once in a while. They also prayed at home. So, Mira had witnessed God at work. However, this battle was personal, and she needed her miracle. One night, while alone in Europe, Mira knelt to pray. After a lengthy, deep, intense, and desperate prayer, she rose from the floor, wiping away the remnants of her tears, and settled to sleep. During this slumber, she had a haunting nightmare depicting the premature passing of her beloved mother after a brief illness. The vision ended with a message: "But seek ye first the kingdom of God, and his righteousness; and all these things shall be added unto you" (Matthew 6:33, King James Version).

She woke up from the dream trembling, but the ending biblical promise brought her comfort. Before going back to sleep, she prayed again, relying on God to keep her mother safe now that she was returning home. Standing on faith, she entrusted her future academics to Him. Encouraged to be with her mother, she gained a new perspective on her brother-in-law's new job; it was a means for God to shift her in the right direction, and not to hurt her.

It was also humbling to realize she had no control over life and surrendering to the Master of time and circumstances (God) was wise. He saved her from drowning in sorrowful tears. Rather than mourning the failed dream, she refocused on the tangible blessings of seeing her family in Europe and taking a break from her community. With this attitude, Mira put her frustration in Switzerland behind her, and later, everything made more sense.

Mira was ready to return to Zaire, but studying there was still out of the question. Unsure why she thought God owed her anything, she prayed,

"God, hasten your plan for me to study abroad. It is on you if you don't open this door for me, and I do something foolish."

She believed in the God of the impossible, transforming her mother, a high-school dropout, and her father, a young boy who sold vegetables, into agents of change. Although their paths differed from hers, she reassured herself that her dream was right up God's alley of wonders. Now, let us return to the flight on her way back!

Just One More Push

The plane landed in Lusaka, the capital of Zambia, in Africa. The next day, Mira did one thing before heading to the border.

"Well, studying in Switzerland didn't pan out! Instead, I can go to America!" She told herself.

She asked the cab driver to stop at the American Embassy in Lusaka so she could try her luck and ask for a visa to the USA. It does not work like that!

She did not make it past the front desk. The Embassy denied her request and stamped her passport. This stamp is the worst nightmare for anyone requiring a visa to travel as it implies 'unfit to enter your country.' For Mira, not getting the visa was less threatening than the near-impossible odds of getting it.

Following her failed attempt, she returned to the cab, drove to the bus station, and headed to the Zambia/Zaire border to hail another taxi to her sister's house for a few days. After that, she made her way to her parents' place. They were happy to see her and maintained a hopeful outlook. The community was the same, except Mira was in the future. Her love for the wild mushrooms from her community, in particular the Terya, remained strong, and she aspired to be like them, embracing her fate and hoping to contribute to the greater good. She grew even closer to her parents and her mother did not die.

PART 3: A NEW DOOR OPENS

The time came and Mira met the Punctual God! "He has made everything beautiful in its time. He has set eternity in the human heart; yet no one can fathom what God has done from beginning to end," Ecclesiastes 3:11 (NIV).

- Story 7: Bound By Faith Farewell
- Story 8: Cultural Contrasts & New Beginnings
- Story 9: Dream Chase and A Warm Surprise

Story 7: Bound By Faith Farewell

A Soulful Prayer

God is good; He answered Mira's bold prayer in Switzerland! A couple of months after returning to Zaire, she started a new phase of her life. This opportunity was not out of the blue.

Mira's parents had laid the foundation for her academic pursuits during their sabbatical in America. Even after their return to Zaire, there was no favorable answer for a while, and Mira was still in Europe. So, the news of acceptance into college was the breakthrough they yearned for. The weight of her shattered dreams lifted, and the future looked hopeful. She packed a small suitcase and was ready to go.

The day to leave came! Mira's mother gathered everyone in the living room for a farewell prayer of gratitude and to anchor the journey in Christ, the solid rock. Mira would be away for at least four years, making this separation from her parents the longest. When she went to Europe, her parents were absent. So, this farewell was even more meaningful. It was her mom's plea for God's covering and their blessings over her as she set out for the United States of America.

Mira's mother, a fervent, praying woman, struggled to hold back tears of joy. Next, she closed her eyes, clasped her hands, and delivered a soulful prayer.

At that moment, the sun's soft golden glow filtered through the white veil, which moved with the wind entering the open windows. Mira, dressed in her modest travel outfit - jeans and a short-sleeved blouse, soaked in the cozy ambiance of God's presence, embracing the birth of a new chapter in her life. She surrendered to God with every word her mother lifted to heaven. Amen!

Hitchhiking Forward

Mira and her family headed towards the sole road linking their small community to the outside world. Do you remember her walking Francois to hitchhike his ride when he broke up with her in Story 4? This was the same place they walked to send off Mira. After a brief wait, a truck pulled up, and Mira hopped in, clueless about what was about to come. As the vehicle drove away and her cherished home disappeared, she traveled back in time, replaying earlier conversations with her mother.

"Mira, would you help me do the laundry?" her mother would ask.

"Sure, mommy!" she would respond.

Her mother would hide money in pockets every time, turning laundry day into a treasure hunt. Other times, they would look through old photo albums, and her mother would reminisce about her younger days. Her beauty and fashion sense would take Mira's breath away, from African wraps to afros, 'Elephant' pants, and platform shoes. However, they would start crying whenever they reached a few photos of Mira's grandfather. He died at the prime of his life and was very close to his daughter. Although they had never met, Mira was eager to learn about the skilled hunter her parents had named her after (a customary practice). Did Mira inherit her tomboy traits from him? It is anyone's guess! However, it was a privilege to embody some of his masculine qualities.

Mira learned so much about her childhood during these conversations. In short, 'Mira was a happy child'. She enjoyed these talks, but interjected when her mother discussed her last wishes. Uncomfortable discussing death, Mira would ask for more cheerful topics. Her mother would go along. However, somehow, Mira learned the song her mother wished her children would sing when she died.

Her eyes welled up with tears recounting these moments. She mustered the courage to wave goodbye again, even though they had disappeared from view. Her mother's voice became the invisible thread that kept them connected.

> "Always remember, I love you," she yelled to Mira before the truck disappeared.

Her father's silence and one-sided smile were integral to his persona, communicating more than words could. He imparted so much wisdom to Mira; she knew he was proud of her. The rest of the family flooded her with so much love she left feeling blessed. Within a couple of hours, the truck arrived at the closest city. She boarded a bus to go spend the night with her other sister. The next day, she met a missionary who offered to help with the travel arrangements, including going to the U.S. Embassy to apply for a visa. Mira and her family were grateful.

The morning came; it was time to go.

Welcome Back to Lusaka

Remember when she came from Switzerland, stopped at the U.S. Embassy, and had her passport stamped at the front desk? That is where they went, stepping into God's paradox. The door that had shut on her before now swung open, propelling her into a promising academic trajectory. She received her visa.

Next, Mira stood in awe at the airport terminal (still in Zambia), knowing God gave her the green light to restart. She boarded the plane, and it took off. Soon enough, the flight attendants offered refreshments, followed by meals. She ate, talked with the person beside her, leaned back against her seat, and slept. Hours later, she boarded her connecting flight. Her mind kept trying to look into the future, but she forced herself to focus on the present moment, thousands of feet suspended between two worlds, to enjoy every moment.

Once again, her parents were right, not that she ever doubted them. God had always been good, and "He who began a good work in you is faithful to complete it" (Philippians 1:6). He did it again for Mira. Filled with a profound sense of obligation, she left the familiar nest behind, vowing to make herself and her parents proud. Her outlook on life and unwavering determination guided her through setbacks, believing anything was achievable with the right mindset and a firm foundation. Hers included a clear vision for the future, respect for her parents, and faith in God through Jesus Christ.

She left her parents' home holding on to two academic dreams and aspiring to become a wife and mother of four children, two girls and two boys.

Story 8: Cultural Contrasts & New Beginnings

Mira's Second Chance

Welcome to the home of opportunity! The state of Maryland, USA, was the starting point of her academic journey, guided by the values etched into her heart. But there was a slight hiccup - she did not speak English! With help, she cleared customs and made her way to the carousel, joining fellow passengers from her flight to retrieve her luggage.

However, the struggle to get through the remaining part of the terminal was real, making the wait for her pickup feel desperate. Her multi-language background was useless; she missed the multiple public announcements calling and instructing her to join the search party. Tired, she dozed off on a bench. Thankfully, her ride located her. When she walked outside, the heat was suffocating, and she broke into a sweat instantly. It was nothing she had ever experienced, even from a tropical country in the heart of Africa.

"Thank goodness for air conditioning in the car." She sighed!

They got stuck in traffic jam. Mira had never seen such a thing. In her small community in Zaire, people depended on one road to connect them beyond their local area, with the nearest major city being 35 kilometers (22 miles) away. She experienced traffic congestion in her homeland and Switzerland; it was nothing like the U.S., where drivers cut each other off to gain a one-car advantage. She found that impatience disturbing. But who cared? She had arrived!

A few days later, she recovered from jet lag and began exploring the surroundings. It was surprising to see so many pedestrians on the streets, and then Mira understood the pleasant weather and that the weekend drew people outdoors. Then, there were 7-Eleven and fast-food establishments.

> Mira wondered, *"why operate 24 hours a day, seven days a week? Do people rest in this country? Why did the monster-sized burgers come with gargantuan drinks?"*

These discoveries, and countless others, were beyond her imagination.

More Shocking Discovery

Mira learned about America from various sources, like movies, history classes, missionaries in her community, and her father's travels. Television portrayed themes of strength, elegance, and entrepreneurship associated with the country. In school, students learned about America as a resilient nation capable of overcoming dark times. Documentaries also praised America as an ideal destination. Even interactions with American missionaries in Zaire left a positive impression on

Mira. Souvenirs her dad brought from America added to her excitement about the country.

However, the harsh reality changed her perception of this great country.

> *"There are people experiencing homelessness and beggars in America? How can they stay safe and warm while living on the streets and under bridges in tents, especially in winter?"* Mira wondered.

> *"There are different kinds of white people?"*

Mira did not know there were distinctive groups, such as Irish, Polish, Italians, and Greeks, and each celebrated their ancestry beyond the USA. In school, she learned about the migration from Europe to America, colonization, and slavery. It always was about one White race. She must have slept through classes and missed a lot.
Nonetheless, the shock continued.

> *"Within the Black race, there were shades of blackness, each connected to beauty or lack of it, and people struggled based on their skin tone?"*

The colonial heritage and its fallout were apparent and awakening.

Beyond racial disparities, Mira often took public transportation to move about. She noticed clean buses with the word 'EXPRESS' pulled up at bus stops. The drivers were so friendly and smiled while greeting every passenger. They smiled even to close the door. Looking at how polished the passengers looked and the quality of customer service, they earned the right to the luxurious commute.

The buses Mira caught were opposite. The drivers would see passengers standing by a puddle and did not try to avoid it, splashing dirty water on anyone too slow to jump back. Desperate riders ran to avoid missing the bus, but it would still take off without waiting a few more seconds. Others arrived behind schedule and turned the 'out of service' sign on, crushing people's hopes. The unequal treatment affirmed that one had to belong to a particular class to receive respect in America.

How was this possible? Mira understood addressing these 'elephants in the room' ruffled feathers so people shy away from it. Her skewed ideology of a 'melting pot' revealed blind spots she did not know existed in the country she joined to build her future. Standing on a principle instilled by her parents: "Fear no one but God, and show respect to everyone," this woman stepped forward, and committed more than ever before to be part of the solution. Fearless and unstoppable, she charged forward.

Story 9: Dream-chase and A Warm Surprise

Lost in Translation & Determined to Excel

English was still challenging for her. So, when school started, she attended orientation, but everything the speaker said in the auditorium was foreign. Yet, she joined in the clapping and laughter of the other peers. It made no difference if she understood any of it. Being on-site at the campus, ready to further her education, was more than fulfilling.

Then, Mira ventured into the well-equipped library at the college. She had seen nothing comparable to it before. In her community in Zaire, the university where her father worked counted most books, and they fit along the walls. His book selection at home came second. He was an avid reader. The primary and secondary schools had no libraries or bookstores. So, students would copy notes from the blackboard. Picture yourself being absent from class and then making up for it.

> *"If my parents achieved so much with modest starts, I have everything necessary to succeed."* Mira reassured herself.

The Path Forward

Mira had her eyes set on two professions. The first was to pursue a career as a physician, inspired by her mom and her other brother-in-law. Her mother assisted many women in childbirth as a midwife and he was a healthcare professional. She wanted to get as close to God's creation as possible and help people heal, as they did, respectively. This ambition ended with no warning. It began with a slight swelling on her middle finger, requiring professional treatment. Her brother-in-law applied numbing medication, and watching the procedure turned out to be traumatic. She fainted. She must have required general anesthesia to sleep through it. That day, her dream of becoming a physician ended.

The alternate choice was to become an engineer. This dream stemmed from her desire to help repair deplorable roads in her homeland. The condition worsened during the rainy season, leaving people without access to basic needs such as schools, hospitals, markets, and much more. Mira wanted to be part of the solution to help families and communities stranded in remote areas. So, off she went to become a civil engineer.

Navigating Academic Horizons

Mira was a quick learner. However, moving from one class to the next building was challenging. Of these new experiences, catching the school bus for the first time to go to a new campus was the most frightening. She was used to public transportation and knew her routes, unlike the school bus, which drove through unfamiliar areas. So, Mira prayed for the entire ride.

Her fear was ironic since she hitchhiked in Zaire. Why was she afraid? In her homeland, the road was two-lane. It winded between villages, and vehicles traveled at stop-and-go speed. Also, travelers did not just jump in any car that stopped; there were safety considerations.

Contrary to America, it seemed probable to transport students elsewhere based on the excellent condition of the roads. Mira's fear of riding with a stranger for the first time heightened from hearing about crime daily on the news and seeing Amber Alerts. She overcame this fear as the other students on the bus seemed comfortable. Some turned out to be her classmates from Ethiopia, Russia, Egypt, France, and India, and they became friends learning English together. She even picked up a few Russian words. She registered for math classes to catch up on lost time in high school and Switzerland. They did not require English proficiency.

Who knew repeating the last year of secondary school would give her an edge in mathematics in America, enabling her to skip a few prerequisites?

Let us step back to Africa for a moment!

In Zaire, students had to select a specific field of study for their final two years of secondary school to graduate. Mira's was math and physics. After failing the State Exam in the first round (Story 4), she immersed herself in studying to pass the following year and did it. The hard work paid off in America. So, taking math in college was a walk in the park, but physics was a different story. Understanding how things move and interact with each other requires language proficiency, so physics would be next after gaining a better lingual grip. Mira charged forward to honor herself and her parents. With God on her side, success was inevitable.

Independence Walls

The day arrived when Mira reached a significant milestone in her schooling journey, moving into a townhouse with her friend. Photographs of their loved ones adorned the walls, reminding them of the sacrifices made to reach this point. Mira, in moments of solitude, would reflect on the humbling journey of her life, the walls echoing the temporary nature of everything, while the floors bore the weight of more steps into adulthood. All the pieces of furniture in the house, carefully chosen from thrift stores, held sentimental value as Mira and her friend embraced a future full of promises.

Two years later, Mira's father surprised her with a visit during his Church Mission. Hosting him for a few days before his return was an incredible honor. As always, he shared his wisdom to remind Mira of her strength and ability to overcome obstacles. During those few days together, he was always awake to wish her well when she left for school. He made omelets and fried plantains, and they would eat before she headed out. Once home, they walked around the neighborhood and visited the town. Every day, he cleaned the dishes.

"That is the least I can do," he would say.

He would stay up to read, and before Mira went to sleep, they would pray, and then he would enrich her with more life wisdom. Their time apart strengthened their bond; even if Mira's mother was absent, they both felt so present. As their few days together ended, Mira did not want to let her father leave. However, she found new determination and strength, fueled by her parents' belief in her abilities to overcome any obstacle. To eternalize his visit, Mira would read over and over the letters her mother and family members wrote. Her sister Delia could not write, so her letters were always part of her mother's. Life had to go on! She continued with her classes and exploring Maryland. While it was fascinating to ride public transportation, during the Wintertime, nothing was exciting. No matter how she bundled up, cold squeezed in somehow, and her Central African nature refused to adapt.

PART 4: IN THE EYE OF THE STORM

"While being strong might seem solitary, it could be the only path available to survive when all else fades."

Hadassah

- Story 10: Unforeseen Welcomes
- Story 11: Taking a Stand
- Story 12: Divine Intervention

Story 10: Unforeseen Welcomes

First Storm

America welcomed Mira until life pulled the rug from under her feet. One day, her friend and roommate informed her she was moving out for better opportunities, and she left before the month ended. Mira understood we do what we must do for ourselves, but the news was still shocking and brought forth a flood of troubling uncertainties. The once-energetic space became desolate, and an unsettling silence replaced the laughter that once echoed. Mira was afraid and helpless, as the rent was too high alone.

> *'What do I do? Where do I go?'* Mira wondered while lying on her bed, tossing and turning.

She could have asked her family for help, but she knew that leaving the comfort of home and venturing into the world for personal growth would be challenging, but rewarding. So, she opted to find a solution on her own. Her savings could not sustain the cost of living for the remaining duration of the lease, which they had renewed. Faced with the daunting wall of the upcoming rents, breaking the lease became the inevitable solution. But where would she go?

She turned to God for help, and faith was all she had as she waited for divine intervention. Reminiscing about people experiencing homelessness on the streets and under bridges, she realized the thin line between having a home and losing it, and no one was immune to it. Then, the Holy Spirit reminded her of the 'collective responsibility.' So, she headed to her church and asked for help. Jehovah Jireh— God the Provider — answered in her favor (AGAIN). Without hesitation, the pastor connected her with Vivienne, a white lady who needed someone to stay with her and do minor chores around the house. The penalty for breaking the lease was still a significant roadblock. Mira did what she knew best, praying, then headed to the leasing office to present her case. After explaining her situation, the receptionist said,

> "We are sorry about what you are going through, but don't worry; just make sure you leave the house clean."

Mira witnessed God's faithfulness once again! They had moved in without a deposit, so she did not expect a refund. She packed, sold a few things, donated the rest, and moved in with Vivienne. It was a splendid arrangement. Vivienne and Mira bonded over watching television, and they would engage in long conversations, which helped Mira put the past behind. She even improved her English skills. Soon enough, Mira got a job within walking distance, working part-time. In addition, Vivienne paid her a small amount for the chores in the house. The new living arrangement helped save most of her earnings.

The two of them grew closer, and Vivienne felt comfortable admitting to having a crush on the news guy.

"If I were young, and he asked me out, I would say yes without hesitating," she said.

They would laugh as she described the man's facial features. He was black. Watching the news became their moments of laughter and bonding as Vivienne looked forward to seeing her self-declared boyfriend on television every night.

Mira continued to believe in her success and was proud to overcome her challenges. No one needed to know about losing her apartment; living with Vivienne was temporary, trusting God had her back. While at work, she met Ethan, and they started dating, bringing her one step closer to becoming a wife and mother of two boys and two girls.

You Did Not Tell Me

Growing up in her homeland, Mira's parents had a simple rule about dating.

"When you meet someone, bring them home to meet us." So, Mira decided to introduce Ethan to Vivienne.

She looked forward to meeting him and joked about continuing to date her journalist. On Saturday morning, the doorbell rang. Mira hurried to let Ethan in. They entered the living room, where

Vivienne had turned off the television to greet him. However, Vivienne appeared startled, her eyes widened, and she frowned. One would think that Vivienne came face-to-face with a phantom.

"Are you ok?" Mira asked.

"Yes, I'm fine," she responded.

Next, she greeted Ethan and excused herself. She got up, grabbed the recliner handle, and retreated to her bedroom until he left about thirty minutes later. As Mira prepared for work, she murmured with disappointment,

"You didn't tell me he was white!"

Mira could not believe her ears! Her stomach flipped upside down, and her heart cringed. She never felt insulted for being black than she did then. That was another dark side of America the world could never imagine possible from the outside. Growing up, her small community hosted white people from all over the world and treated them like royalty out of hospitality. It was a rude awakening to her skewed perception about race, and Mira was furious.

> "This white woman was in love with and professed her love for a black journalist she met on television every evening. How dared-she? I've been living with a racist for months now and didn't even know. How did she think of me as I cleaned the house?"

59

Then she turned to God, *"Why would you allow me to lose my apartment to land in this hypocrisy?"*

More rage and anger built up within her as her brain downloaded more questions, but she internalized everything and would go to work and school, anticipating the worst. Such blatant racism and insincerity could not be all the evil there was. Mira felt uneasy returning to Vivienne's house after work. But she had nowhere else to go.

Soon enough, Vivienne began enforcing strict protocols on Mira, making the situation even more unbearable.

> "Do not use the washer and dryer; the bill is too high. Don't eat my food; I need it to take my medication. Turn the light off in your room; you are wasting energy."

The list of restrictions grew longer. Vivienne eventually asked Mira to return the house key. Mira could not enter the house for hours. She unlocked the door a few minutes before her sister, Loretta's, scheduled to visit. Could she stay away until Loretta scheduled visits to her sister? No! Mira was still under a verbal agreement to be present when not at school or at work.

Stranded In Solitude

Someone once said: "A drowning man will clutch at a straw." Mira lost her apartment, and Vivienne was her sole shelter. Her part-time yielded insufficient income to sustain essentials like rent, bills, food, bus passes, and other basic needs. Against her will, she swallowed her pride and endured the pain of staying where she was unwanted. The plan was to persevere until the end of the school semester in December, allowing herself time to devise a solution.

Meanwhile, Vivienne kept locking Mira outside the house. Mira did not care; the weather was warm. To kill time, she would walk around the neighborhood admiring butterflies, birds, and color-changing leaves. While appreciating God's artistic work, she saw houses with beautiful plants and would tear up. The well-maintained front yard reminded Mira of her mother. She loved gardening.

She also ran into neighbors, and they would hold small talks, which were breaths of fresh air sweeping as she took advantage of the good time away from Vivienne. There were also children playing, and it reconnected her to a carefree childhood in Africa. Mira enjoyed every outdoor delight while killing time. There was more than enough to keep her unconcerned about being locked out. Then Winter came.

It became brutal to stay stranded outside as the cold weather settled in. Mira grew up in the heart of Africa, where the equator divided her country in two. Her struggle with the cold was real! The outdoors, once a source of comfort, now became unbearable, enveloping her in loneliness. One day,

Loretta, Vivienne's sister, stopped by the house and found Mira shivering on the doorstep. Puzzled, she asked why. Mira downplayed her predicament. Loretta opened the door. When they walked in, Vivienne pretended to be asleep. Then the sisters walked into the bedroom.

On the way out, Loretta's demeanor had changed. Left to speculate on what Vivienne might have disclosed, Mira feared the worst, and she was right. She spent more time stranded outside, and Loretta's visits became infrequent. Days became gloomier. Praying is all she could do while enduring.

Defrosting Frozen Hope

One day, while opening the back door for her dog, Angela, a kind 90-year-old neighbor, noticed Mira sitting on the stairway again. They engaged in small talk through the fence, and as time passed, Angela invited Mira to join her in her backyard. The more time they spent together, the more she became comfortable asking Mira to help around the house, such as making sandwiches, getting her something to drink, and feeding the dog, Gold. Helping Angela brought back the beautiful memories of Mira and her grandparents in Africa. Their connection provided them with mutual support, and they saw each other daily, becoming closer as time passed and marking the end of Mira freezing on the doorstep. Mira never shared what went on with

Vivienne. Ethan, Mira's boyfriend, knew nothing about it neither; it was a tiny bump on the road.

One evening, Mira noticed the dog was not in the backyard as usual and went to see Angela to check. In tears, she said: "Gold died last night." Mira was sad. Over the time spent together, she also became attached, but her pain was not near what Angela felt. They spent years, just the two of them. So, Gold's death took a toll on her, and she became ill soon after, requiring full-time in-house care. Mira tried several times to visit Angela and was told that only family members could see her. After losing connection with Angela, Mira found it challenging to deal with Vivienne and considered seeking help from the church. She hesitated. The pastor who helped her before was no longer there. Also, the potential repercussions on Vivienne and Loretta were too high; they attended the church too.

Exhausted, Mira confided in her boyfriend. He offered her temporary shelter, but moving in with him went against her beliefs, and she feared it would dishonor her parents. On the other end, staying with Vivienne was killing her. So, against her belief, she agreed to move in with him and kept it a secret, finding solace in knowing her parents loved Ethan and his family loved her. Also, Mira believed they had a future together. So, eventually, she would tell her parents. At that moment, it was a matter of surviving the storm, and Ethan offered shelter.

Mira wanted to say goodbye to Angela before leaving, but she was not sure if she could see her. When Mira explained who they were to each other and that she was moving away, Angela's caregiver asked her to wait. She returned and allowed Mira to see her friend. Angela did not recognize her. It was a poignant reminder of how unpredictable and fleeting life can be. This realization removed all the sting from Mira's experiences with Vivienne. She reminded herself everything would fade away. If she could not change it, it was an unnecessary burden to bear. With that in mind, Mira packed her belongings and was ready to move out.

Breaking Silence for Liberation

Mira told Vivienne she was moving out.

"When?" Vivienne asked.

"This week," Mira replied.

They had not spoken to each other in a while, and the air was thick, unveiling the irreparable state of their relationship. Ethan arrived in his SUV on the weekend, and they loaded her belongings into the truck. Mira said goodbye.

Do you remember the recliner Vivienne got up from when Ethan walked into the house?

She was sitting there, and for the first time, Mira detected an unsettling sadness in her eyes.

"Was it fear? Was mistreating Mira easier than letting her go? Or was Vivienne hoping for redemption, banking on Mira to stick around to help deal with her demons?" Mira wondered in silence.

She also empathized, but it was time to go. She did not deserve Vivienne's treatment, nor could she endure more cruelty. Mira still adhered to her parents' dating rule of introducing friends to the family, but she changed it to include a warning. "Bring your friends home for everyone to meet, but remember that someone letting you into their life does not make them family. Do not get too comfortable."

Mira did not know Vivienne and introducing Ethan to her unveiled her true character. She figured out the hard way that Vivienne was polite but never cared for her. And there is a significant difference between courtesy and ingenuity. Despite the challenges of losing her apartment, facing racism, and life's fragility with Angela, Mira found the strength within herself to keep moving. Each step was critical; hope was her secret weapon to walking with her head held high. She worked hard to keep her inner light shining and refused to let it extinguish, believing that the world could slap her and even throw her off balance, but she could only feel as trapped as she allowed it.

Story 11: Taking a Stand

Dancing Through Adversity

Mira sought refuge with her boyfriend for a few months. He would drop her off, pick her up from school, and even teach her how to drive. Ethan loved cooking, so Mira only spent a little time in the kitchen. Whatever she wanted, he provided. They were both family-oriented and traditional. So, when Ethan introduced her to his parents over the phone, and they came to visit, Mira believed the future together was promising. She even shared with him the dowry tradition in Africa, which involved offering a symbolic gift to honor her parents. They planned to travel to Africa for this event, and Mira looked forward to Ethan meeting her family. However, things changed.

His work schedule was crazy enough, but he started spending even more time away, which left little room for emotional connection, and their relationship suffered the consequences. The decline of their affection rendered the secret of living together heavy. Self-reproach made praying more difficult. So, she turned to music to cope. One of her favorite songs was "Hold On" by Wilson Phillips. The lyrics were therapeutic as she held onto school, the only stable aspect of her life since arriving in America. Realizing that she could not compete with his dedication to work, their relationship fell apart. Ethan's two amazing dogs became her pillars of strength. They witnessed her heartbreak in silence.

Mira could not take it anymore. She confided in her parents about things not working out and that she would break up with him. They were sad, and so was Mira, but being lonely in a relationship was too much to bear. Her parents supported her decision and encouraged her to stay strong, focus on school, and trust God. With music, dance, two amazing dogs, and supportive parents, Mira accepted it was over. Did her parents know they lived together? We will never know.

It was a friendly breakup. Ethan even helped her find an affordable studio in the City's heart of Baltimore. She had a job and savings so she could afford to pay rent. The train stop was within walking distance. Armed with her newfound independence, Mira stood alone for the first time in America, still committed to her academic dream of becoming an engineer. The struggles she faced were integral to her growth.

A Sanctuary of Growth and Healing

Mira settled into her studio, which was flooded with sunlight through enormous windows, reigniting her passion for the garden. She filled her living space with tropical plants as a tribute to her mother, who had given her a green thumb. These plants were beautiful. One would think they were artificial. Caring for them would take Mira back home to her childhood, which warmed her heart.

> *"If I could care for myself as I do these plants and stand tall amid storms, my life will soon bloom,"* Mira told herself.

Her studio was more than just a place to live; it was a sanctuary where Mira could forget life's troubles and focus on personal growth. With her mattress on the floor, she could pray again, and nothing convicted her. It was her, her dream, and God.

Ethan stayed in touch with Mira, tried to reconcile, and even proposed marriage. When they were still together, Mira fell in love with a house on a large piece of land where she could grow food and flowers. Ethan bought Mira's dream house to reignite their passion. That was nice, but not enough; Mira had already received so many gifts from him. She longed for his love, but at that point, her heart was unwilling to go back. Her emotional scars ran deep; no diamond ring could erase them, and no house could mend her broken heart. In the end, Ethan married another African girl who moved into the house. That part was unsettling, but she put it behind her. After her six-month lease ended, Mira renewed it for an entire year and continued enjoying stability and security. She missed her family.

> *"I guess that's the price to pay for following your dreams,"* Mira reflected.

In these quiet moments, her journey was one of rebirth.

A Cliffhanger

Mira was doing great, but life reserved another undeserved surprise for her. She went to work as usual. Then they called her into the office to tell her the company was downsizing, and she was on the chopping block!

With no more income, her savings depleted in the blink of an eye, leaving her unable to keep up with her expenses. Soon enough, she received an eviction notice, which marked the third time she was on the verge of homelessness. Her school did not allow her to work, except during the summer, which left her unsure about her future. Only one person could help her, expecting nothing in return: Ethan. When she contacted him, he assisted without hesitation and spoke to the landlord, securing a one-month extension to the eviction date. It helped but could not keep her warm. She lost electricity because of unpaid bills. She contemplated dragging her mattress into the kitchen and sleeping closer to the oven to stay warm. However, this extreme measure was not worth risking the lives of everyone in the building, including herself. Instead, she layered up in clothing and sought refuge in prayer, which was not easy.

Each moment in God's presence fueled her anger, so she put Him on trial again.

> "What kind of Loving Father leads his child on unstable grounds, with each step pointing to more uncertainties?"

As Mira grappled with her feelings of injustice and despair, she questioned her faith and the fairness of God. The contrast between those who took shortcuts and succeeded and those who did what was right left her contemplating quick answers.

> "Do you want me to take shortcuts to make money? My parents and family are too far from America, and they trust that all is well with me, but that is far from true. What do you want from me?" She yelled to God.

Drenched in tears, Mira wrestled with helplessness, holding the eviction notice to her heart as she watched the month Ethan paid for slip away with each passing day.

In the Valley of Shadows

Mira stood at a crossroads, responding to an ad promising quick earnings with no experience required. After enduring the subsequent interview, she got the job working under a pseudonym; we will leave it at that! That day unfolded her worst nightmare.

The night preceding the appointment, restless thoughts plagued Mira as she tossed and turned in the weight of terror. With a heavy heart, the next day dawned, entangled in a whirlwind of emotions—fear, shame, desperation, and countless others. On her knees, she cried out to God, questioning His plan:

"Is selling my soul the vision you have for your daughter?" Her wavering faith kept God on trial.

Mira watched the clock tick away, and the driver pulled outside her apartment. It was already dark. The sight of the waiting cab from her second-floor studio sent her heart racing with trembling and agony. She descended two flights of stairs and stepped into the cab, longing for a divine intervention that seemed out of reach.

'I'm going, and it's all your fault!' she muttered in resentment, blaming God for the situation she put herself in.

As she continued the internal, one-sided talk, God remained silent. Fear of the unknown awaiting her on the other side of this journey pierced her soul, paralyzing her. Self-convicting thoughts flooded her mind. She silenced them but running to God for rescue seemed unsuccessful. The cab driver peeked in the rear-view mirror and said,

"We are almost there. You will stay in the car until I give you further directions."

Mira was in tears and continued her desperate plea to God, filled with regret over her decision. They reached their destination. The driver exited the taxi, leaving her alone. Two imposing figures stood inside the door on the second floor, arguing with the driver.

These men towered over him, and their angry gestures caused their long hair to whip around like a tempest-ravaged forest. Her anxiety heightened. Mira was alone, feeling abandoned, and dreading the potential consequences of this risky venture. In her darkest moment, she needed a Savior. The cab driver rushed down the stairways, entered the car, slammed the door shut, and started the engine to bring her back. Trapped in the nightmare, Mira gathered her courage to ask,

"What happened?"

The driver was mad, and his response struck her like lightning, reviving her.

"You are Black. They don't want a black person anymore. They want an Asian girl. If you knew you did not want to be here, you should not have wasted our time," he added.

Mira cared less about the driver. She was a living miracle. God protected her, but left Mira to experience the power and consequences of her reckless decisions and actions. He showed up on time and killed the seed of damnation and self-blame before it grew by disrupting the plan. Not like with Vivienne, who made her feel beneath her being black and dating a white man; in this situation, her BLACKNESS was her shield against the two men standing in the doorway, what laid behind the door, and the aftermath. Before she was born, God established her in that skin color as a wall of protection.

Reflecting on her journey, she embraced a deeper relationship with the God of the impossible. She even realized, yes, shortcuts could yield quick answers painting pretty pictures, but at what price? Nothing was worth losing her soul. As she continued reflecting on her descent into a dark pit and the fear leading up to it, it was clear she was a product of grace and mercy to have escaped with only scars of terror.

She pledged never to tread such a path again, fearful that God might withdraw His intervention in future desperation. That night, she bathed, ate the leftovers in the fridge, and praised God. Layered in clothes to stay warm, she slept like a baby, knowing she had met the Lord, her Sheppard. He left the thousand to find her when she went astray. With no judgment, He gave her a blank canvas to repaint her life.

The eviction notice was still by her bed; its threat diminished. Standing in faith, Mira trusted that the same God who guided her through dark valleys would be the comforting rod and staff leading her forward. Her plants still needed care despite the uncertainty of staying in the studio, so she tended to them with care. The mattress remained on the floor, now serving as a humble altar for her prayers. Though the studio remained chilly, Mira was grateful to stay alive and pushed forward.

Within a week before the end of the month, Mira received a job offer as a math tutor at her school. In her moments of desperation and searching for a solution, God had already paved a path for her. With renewed hope, she caught up on her rent, tore the eviction notice, restored power in her studio, and found more reasons to count her blessings.

It dawned on Mira that with God, it comes down to patience. Yes, the likelihood of losing housing was frightening, but she learned the hard way to trust God instead of being quick to jump to conclusions and make decisions out of desperation.

Story 12: The Unforeseen

Peaceful and Joyful Rides

Mira still lived in peace in her studio in Baltimore City, and her lease became month-to-month, allowing her the freedom to move out anytime. This journey of liberation was a harsh awakening, forcing her out of hiding. She began reaching out to her family more often. There was no need to struggle alone. Her family was ready and willing to help anytime.

In the third year since coming to America, she met Greg at school. They loved the outdoors, so weekend adventures became routine—road trips, visits to the zoo, hikes, canoeing, camping, and many more activities. The trips to the zoo were among her favorites. They brought up happy memories of her homeland when her only responsibility was to be free and happy. The future seemed promising, and Mira still hoped to get married and have children.

While her studio, close to the train station, facilitated her daily commutes, some of her classes and tutoring hours were nighttime. The lurking shadows, cars with tainted windows stopping along the street after sunset, and the amounts of reported crimes forced her to move out to a one-bedroom apartment in a safer area. The windows were smaller than those from her studio. However, she traded lighting for the view of deer and their white-spotted fawns in her backyard from her second floor. It was breathtaking, as Mira loved nature and looked forward to their visits. Their presence reassured her that the future was still bright, rebirth was part of life cycles, and God was watching over her. Between Greg picking her up and the bus stop near her home, Mira could move around.

Foolish Decision?

Their relationship was going great. After a year of dating, they discussed marriage. Greg even looked for engagement rings. They agreed they could find a diamond ring with more carats for the same amount if they purchased it outside America. Mira, approaching her thirties, convinced herself,

> "With such a promising future ahead of us, why not change the order of events?"

She got pregnant before marriage. Everything was fine at the beginning; they planned to get pregnant. However, she was unprepared for the aftermath.

Do you remember the collective responsibility in her homeland in story 1?

Many of those who knew her in America also knew Mira's parents. Yes, the world was that small. However, rather than support as it was back in the day, people took themselves to judge and mock her. Mira getting pregnant was an act of shame in Africa, especially with her parents being well respected. As if the mocking was not asphyxiating enough, Greg and Mira began having heated arguments, often around other women. His phone rang every two seconds, which drove her crazy. They always walked holding hands, but that became uncomfortable as it felt like being put on a leash that he yanked every time a man looked at Mira, turning into reasons to pick fights. God forbid, her phone rang! Mira felt trapped.

This time, Mira did not just keep her parents out; she disappeared from them and everyone else, refusing to answer phone calls, missing classes, and sleeping. In the end, she stopped working to care for the baby in her womb. To minimize emotional distress, Mira enrolled in another school. By then, she had made multiple emergency trips to the hospital on threats of miscarriages.

One day, she was rear-ended, and her pregnant stomach slammed into the steering wheel. While in the ambulance, she called him, but that did not turn out well. The conversation went south, as his priority was the increased car insurance costs. The whole situation was ugly and frightening. While lying in that tiny hospital bed alone, a nurse walked in and said,

> "Your baby's heart is distressed; you need to take care of yourself."

That wake-up call was what she needed. Her baby did not ask to be conceived; it was Mira's responsibility to protect her unborn child, and she did just that, avoiding arguments.

This decision was also conducive for Mira. She never saw her parents argue, so fighting was not her nature. It was draining, and she did not like the person she was becoming.

Mira Holding On

Mira held on for herself and the baby, silently praying that someone would show up to journey with her. Then, one day, the phone rang, and she answered. Greg was away. It was her sister in France. Fear of her sister finding out she was pregnant raced through her mind, but it was subdued with the overwhelming joy that God answered her silent prayer.

> "Are you OK? I had a dream and saw you trapped, crying for help in a dark room. Are you OK?" she asked.

> "Yes, I am fine," Mira responded.

> "The dream felt real. You are lying to me; you would not lie to me. Are you lying to me? I felt the urge to call you. Now tell me the truth," she continued.

At that point, Mira wept.

> "Mira, do you want me to come? You know I will get on the flight if necessary; just say the word!"

Her sister insisted, but Mira needed that conversation, which made her feel less alone.

"No, it's OK. I can handle this and feel much better already," Mira told her sister.

She was happy to be pregnant but not ready to face her family yet. So, she mentioned nothing about the baby or the tension between her and Greg. Her sister prayed and encouraged her to stay strong, promising to check on her more often. She did, and Mira would pick up the phone. Her call was a divine intervention. Mira needed a safe environment to cry and release the pressure built from their dysfunctional relationship.

It had been a while since Mira breathed. So, the calls lift blocks of bricks sitting on her chest. They became buffers protecting the unborn child from crashing under the pressure of her parents' toxic relationship. One thing was for sure: she knew she could count on God's covering when everything else failed. She continued avoiding arguments, though not always successful, but focused on peace, knowing that her baby's safety depended on it.

The baby was not the reason she stayed with Greg. She was in love and the continuing discussions about marriage and having more children misled her into unfounded hope. She also convinced herself shopping for baby clothes together and planning to buy a house affirmed their togetherness. Therefore, she needed to stay and weather the storms of outside interferences. This train of thought made dismissing all the red flags easier than facing the fact that she headed straight into a wall. She knew there was no relationship but lacked the fortitude to break up. Her false perception of love foolishly blinded her as she sunk into the pit of false hope. By the time her eyes opened, she was in too deep.

A Saving Scary Visit

Mira received news her father was coming to the U.S. for the second time and would stop to see her for two weeks before returning to Africa. She was excited! But how would she conceal the pregnancy? Morning sickness and the pregnancy glow were too obvious. It was short of a miracle how the nausea stopped when he arrived. They explored various attractions during his visit, toured the town, and went shopping.

It was summer but forget about the scorching heat. Mira wore a jacket while going out and a hoodie in the apartment to conceal her pregnancy. She would leave for school, return, and nap, attributing her tiredness to schoolwork. So, her father would fry eggs and plantain or make toast for them, or they would eat the leftovers that day. He will then share his wisdom, and they will go to sleep. Her dad became a physical buffer of protection, preventing tension between Greg and Mira and a breeze of fresh air in the apartment. Days flew by, Greg and Mira drove him to the airport to catch his flight to the DRC. In a few days, Mira received a call from her mother.

> "Your father told me you might be pregnant. I am coming to help you care for the baby so you can continue with school."

She did not allow Mira the time to respond. Her call was to kill self-condemnation and fears about her parents rejecting her. Her mother's immediate support filled her with an indescribable sense of release. Her few words soothed her bruised heart from people's mockery. "A mother is a mother," as they say in Africa, and Mira's was rare. She restored a smile to her daughter's face and gave her the strength to face tomorrow without worrying.

Mira wondered why her father said nothing about her pregnancy. Later, she realized he respected her privacy and gave her space to share the news with him when she was ready. Their reunion was about reconnecting and not prying into her personal life. Talking to her mother that day was a turning point for Mira. Her comfort and support helped her overcome fears and anxieties, and she was excited about the future with her mother coming to care for her grandchild.

During their conversation, the baby moved into her womb. It must have been exciting to meet Grandma (Kambo in Swahili)! They moved into a two-bedroom apartment to have more space to host her mother. Mira stood tall again, blessed to have such supportive and loving parents. The call dismantled the crippling fear of rejection, and Mira found herself.

Part 5: MIRA KEPT MOVING

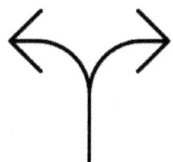

- Story 13: The Shift
- Story 14: The Time Came
- Story 15: Journey to the Past

Story 13-The Shift

Frozen Moments

The weight of shame lifted off her shoulders. She felt unstoppable at the thought of her mother joining them from Africa to babysit her grandchild. One phone call from her reversed the sting of shame and fear, helping Mira regain her mental and emotional posture and fortitude. As they waited for her arrival, she continued going to school on a reduced schedule to minimize stress on the baby and herself, confident about their beautiful future.

One evening, Mira finished her late class and headed to the parking lot, about 10 minutes away on campus. Battling exhaustion and freezing temperatures, she sought to reach her car as quickly as possible, with no desire to engage with Greg. Yet, as usual, he called to keep her company. These calls were reassuring. They eased any anxieties and fears of walking alone at night, and Mira looked forward to them as they reminded her of the caring man she fell in love with. That night, his voice was the last thing she wanted to hear.

Mira refused to pick up. Earlier, the house phone in the kitchen had rung late at night. Greg woke up to answer but missed it, sparking an argument and accusing Mira of unfaithfulness. His people called him on the cell phone and Mira's family on the landline, which had no caller ID. So, they were not on good terms when she left for school later that day.

Fearing another round of tension, a knot of distress tightened in her chest, and she resolved to avoid him and told herself, *"Whatever happens, happens when I get to the apartment."* Mira's striving for peace was in vain. He persisted, and Mira, still reluctant, answered. It was total silence on the other end of the line, and Mira was getting frustrated as she repeated, 'Hello. Are you going to say something?'

As Mira reached the quiet, empty parking lot, she almost hung up on him to disconnect from his mind game. Little did she know her world would flip upside down, changing her forever. With an unsettling calmness, he said,

"It's your mother."

"What do you mean, my mother?" Mira asked, stunned!

"She's gone." He responded.

"What do you mean, gone?"

The news was a chilled encounter with fate. Her world froze and collapsed before her eyes, and Mira wanted the ground to swallow her so she could go with her mother. However, trapped in emotional turmoil and grappling with grief and the impending new life within her, she realized those thoughts were selfish. Gathering her strength, she made it to the car, struggling to process the heartbreaking news.

"The call I missed early morning was from my mother, and now she is dead? The apartment is full of beautiful plants, reminding me of our time together. Would those now be a display of your short-lived life? You promised to help raise your grandchild; what should I tell her? Why did you deny Stella the right to meet you? You lied to me. How am I supposed to go on without you?"

As more questions filled her heart, she felt lost at the thought of never seeing her mother again. She had never felt such excruciating pain and would not wish it even on her worst enemy.

In the past, her mother would talk about her funeral, but Mira found the topic too dark and would always change it. However, this time, she had to confront the inevitable heartbreak and sing the sad song her mother taught her as a child to sing at her funeral. As she sang for her mother thousands of miles in America, each word chipped away a piece of her heart. Cemeteries were frightening as a child! Now, she would have to go to the grave to feel closer to her mother.

In the past, Mira would run to God for His intervention. This time, praying was the last thing on her mind as she drove back to the apartment, angry with God for taking her mother away. Her heart wanted to jump out of her chest as she blamed her mother for choosing Heaven over her offspring. Then there was Greg. Mira resented him. When he moved in, she tip-toed around the house to avoid confrontations. Mira had nothing to hide yet looked over her shoulder, ensuring she did not offend him. She made herself invisible to get by instead of embracing life to the fullest. Replaying the missed phone call earlier, the subsequent arguments, and a quick glance at the prison she locked herself in, staying in a dead relationship fed Mira's bitterness toward Greg.

> *"If I responded, someone could have informed me she was sick. I could have prayed for her, and since God always responds in my favor, she could still be alive. If not, she could have at least said goodbye."*

The line between convicting herself and grieving was thin. The emotional turmoil skewed toward guilt, leading Mira down the path of self-blame. She realized that toxicity led to more anxiety, and she shifted her thought process, owning her part of responsibility.

> *"Missing that call was not all Greg's fault; I chose not to answer. Greg may have set an uncomfortable environment, but I bowed down,"* she murmured.

> *"I was the one who silenced the warrior in me in the name of love and loving Greg. He did not make me do it,"* she continued.

Mira realized how much she had compromised to accommodate their relationship, which revolted her even more. Convinced that the earlier call was from her mother and observing how lost she was in the name of love, something inside her shifted away from Greg. Her mother had been her pillar of strength, and she hoped to take care of her mother one day. Not only did this become impossible, but Mira also had to live with the last memory of her mother from what she heard:

> "She looked like she was sleeping in the coffin with a beautiful smile."

It must be what Heaven does to those who die in Christ. Yet, it felt like hell losing her, but not going to the funeral somehow made it feel unreal.

What Happened?

Mira's parents planned to drop off her passport application in anticipation of babysitting her grandchild in America. She felt a chill in the morning and sat under the sun to warm up, a custom in Africa, especially during cold seasons. While outside with her husband, she shared her dream of singing with angels the previous night; he smiled and replied, "You and your dreams." She stopped at a nearby clinic for a simple checkup before they proceeded with their planned activities. Unfortunately, the situation escalated quickly, and she needed medical attention from a more prominent clinic. Unable to bear watching doctors' failing attempts to find a vein in his wife's arm, he stepped out of the room to breathe. Not long after, doctors called him back; Mira's mom had taken her last breath. What started as a simple desire to warm up under the sun was the last time Mira would ever feel the warmth of her mother's heart and her soothing and graceful voice. Stella will never know Kambo.

Mira pleaded to wake up from the nightmare, only to realize her eyes were wide open and everything was real.

Legacy of Love and Echoes of Strength

Mira's mother was extraordinary. Even in her last moments, she remained considerate, choosing a leap year to leave, sparing her children from yearly mourning. In grieving, Mira believed her mom was still alive as a guardian angel for her loved ones.

Looking back, the day Mira left for America, starting with hitchhiking, her mom said as the truck drove away,

> "I may not see you again. So, always remember, I love you."

She knew her days were being counted. The dream in Switzerland about her mom's death following a temporary sickness only foretold the inevitable fate that awaited.

This 51-year-old indomitable woman had been married for over 36 years at her death. She treated her husband, Mira's dad, like a king and now made him a widower who had to figure out how to move on. She left behind orphans who still needed love and care, and Stella would never feel her grandma's warmth again.

This sudden and immense loss shifted Mira's life views to prioritize and maximize time. Taking a heartbeat for granted became out of the question. Her mother's passing shook Mira to the core.

However, she remained baby Stella's lifeline in the womb, and her mother would have wanted her to stay strong. So, Mira had only one option left—to pick herself up, and she did just that!

She was still envious of Heaven for having regained a star, leaving a dark spot in her heart. All she could do was keep going and embrace the fleeting nature of life. Indeed, "vanity of vanities; all is vanity" (Ecclesiastes 1:2). Decades later, Mira continued to feel the void of losing her mother, and nothing and no one could fill it.

> *"We never get over losing our loved ones; we learn to coexist with the void,"* Mira concluded.

Story 14: The Time Came

Stella and A Special Visit

It had been almost forty days since her mother's passing. Mira still grappled with grief as the wounds of sorrow remained raw. Then, Stella was born, a perfect gift from God. Filled with indescribable, unconditional, and incorruptible love, the room for mistakes tightened as Mira held her newborn baby. Stella, Mira, and Greg left the hospital on the third day. He put the baby in the car seat, and Mira joined in the back, admiring the perfect miracle God allowed her to have. It was one of Mira's best days. Then they reached the main road. Hell broke loose.

Greg unleashed his rage on Mira. She ducked while clutching the baby car seat, but there was only so much hiding place in a sports vehicle. Mira, trapped, cried all the way to the apartment, contemplating dark thoughts as the car drove on the highway. But there was Stella. After a few more name-calling, Greg calmed down and said,

"You did not think I would find out your boyfriend came to visit?"

Here is what happened.

Mira had forgotten a detail about the past. One day, before the baby was born and after Mira's mom's death, Greg accused (again) Mira of cheating on him and lost it. Cornered, tired, unapologetic, and needing air to breathe, she shouted,

"The baby is not even yours."

Let us just say it was ugly in the apartment that day! Fast forwarding to the hospital, Mira had called Ethan to announce she had become a mother, and he came to visit at the hospital. When Greg saw the name signed at the front desk, Mira believed he remembered her false, cruel paternity claim in the past and lost his mind.

She wanted to celebrate motherhood with someone. Based on the incident in the car, Mira wished Ethan never checked in at the hospital's front desk, and she never intended to tell Greg about it. Nothing good could have come out of it, and her fear proved correct. As promised, he did a DNA test, but she had nothing to worry about. She never cheated on him.

Within a couple of months of baby Stella's birth, Mira, still a part-time student, went to the clinic for a checkup for body aches, fatigue, chest pain, etc. The symptoms were ongoing for a few days and worsened. The nurse said it was meningitis, and she went to the hospital. Once there, the situation escalated quickly. The doctors told her she had a severely enlarged heart, and needed to be on the list for a heart transplant. The doctor told Greg first, and when they walked in to deliver the news to Mira, they asked her to say goodbye to Stella. She did not have long to live, unless there was a miracle.

They called the helicopter to transfer her to another hospital. But securing one would take longer than driving.

So, the Ambulance rushed her to the next hospital. It was the scariest day of her life to see her infant as an orphan. Mira was not ready. Greg contacted Mira's family to let them know. She knew they prayed for her as she did for herself. The next ten days in the hospital, including walking rehabilitation, were miraculous. She returned home and did not need a heart transplant. God healed her. The situation went from simple body aches to learning how to walk. Had it not been for God, where would Mira be.

From that point on, every decision and action carried the immense weight of responsibility for herself and the precious creation in her arms. With newfound purpose and meaning in her life, something within herself had to die for them to live. So, Mira began restructuring her life. She ended tolerance for foolishness. With the death of her mother losing its sting with time and gratitude for her life, Mira found more strength to recharge her inner warrior to fight for herself. Greg remained a wild card on Mira's self-healing and personal growth journey. So, prayer was her solution. God orchestrated another visit from her father in no time, the blows dampening the buffer.

Stella Meets Kambo

He arrived, and Mira was over the moon. It did not take long for Grandpa (Kambo) and Stella to bond. She rode on his back, and they played together on the carpet. Stella loved to kiss his bald head. Mira's dad, a book lover, would read to Stella, going through books over and over. After feeding his granddaughter, they would go for a walk and then to the playground for hours. Stella would come back crying every time, wanting to play some more. Grandpa, tired, would still carry her on his shoulder on their way back to the apartment. It was time for him to wake up whenever Stella woke up in the morning. At the gentle nudge of a toddler, he would get ready and repeat yesterday's excitements every day.

Although short, his visit was a blessing that everything would be okay. His presence also made up for Stella's grandmother's absence. When he left, Mira was grateful for the time God allowed them to share, which deepened her sense of peace, helped mend her torn spirit and regain normalcy. Even though there was still more inner healing, being with her father expedited the progress.

A Tough Decision

Mira's and Greg's arguments escalated after her father left. He became blunter in his wrongdoing, to say the least, and Mira could not take it any longer; she needed her sanity. Two years after the birth of their baby, Mira asked him to leave, making the painful and heartbreaking decision to end their relationship. Not only did she love him, but she also hoped to build their future together. Raising a child alone was not in Mira's wildest imagination; they planned to marry. But there is much more to building a home than *feeling love* for someone. Was it even love? Mira questioned herself. It might have started that way, but it turned into a collection of brokenness, and every day felt like navigating a minefield. Breaking up was the best path for the baby, herself, and Greg. Had they stayed together, their relationship would have been a time-ticking bomb, and it was a matter of time before the worst happened.

The decision to leave was costly for Mira, as Greg's departure left her unstable. He was the sole provider. He also promised to take her to court, pulling her into mental and emotional turmoil and threatening to take their child Stella away from her. Drained, Mira feared the worst, as she had no income to prove to the court that she could care for their child. But God stepped in again to wipe away her tears.

He arranged for Mira to run into an acquaintance she had met at church while living with Vivienne over six years ago. They played catch-up, and Mira invited her over. She shared pictures of her family, and they talked for hours. Her children were all grown. Then, Mira shared her concerns, and this good Samaritan reassured her that in Maryland, she would get full custody of her child unless Greg could prove her an unfit mother.

In the end, Mira understood why Greg pressured her to sign the paper and give up custody. His accusations were unfounded, and he relied on her fear of not knowing her right to give up on her daughter. But God the Planner watched over Mira and the child the whole time. Looking back, while Mira was going through it with Vivienne, God established that connection for Mira to meet that good Samaritan, knowing that fast forwarding, she would be Mira's answered prayer and deliver the victory she needed to keep her daughter. Mira found more reasons to worship Yahweh, who orchestrated the breakthrough before even Mira met Greg.

Knowing her rights put Mira at ease, and she celebrated her victory, standing in faith while trusting God to work out the details. Lacking money to care for her daughter was still an issue, but being poor did not make her maternal love questionable. She won Stella's custody without ever setting foot in court or spending money she did not have on lawyers. God was their judge. She could have pursued legal action against Greg for acceptable child support but chose not to, whispering,

> *"The God who guided us through every hurdle will take care of us."*

After Greg left, Mira missed him and contemplated getting back together. However, she also knew that no amount of love could repair the profound damage that had been done. Mira could not risk falling into old patterns of being a shadow again and dragging her child with her. There were too many irreconcilable differences. It was over, and she refused to undermine the healing process. It was one thing to fight for her relationship and another to go back on her decision, which would have been stepping on a sleeping volcano. Entrusting her destiny to God, she embraced the challenge of single motherhood in a foreign land with no job or degree and forged ahead.

God Did It Again!

Mira struggled to forge the path forward, and it was frightening. However, hiding and isolating herself were no longer viable options, as she had done every time she faced adversity. It was impossible anyway. She was alone then; this time, there was Stella, and they lived with the family, who joined to help while Mira worked to figure out the next steps. Greg may have been the sole provider when they were together, but Mira was never alone. She called her sister- and brother-in-law in Europe for help. They stepped up and gave her money without hesitation to cover over six months' rent, easing her concerns about losing her apartment. She then focused on finishing her studies.

Through it all, she spared her father the details to protect him. On his most recent visit, doctors diagnosed him with an incurable heart condition.

Nothing good could come out of overwhelming him with negative news. Mira wanted him to remember his great time in America, especially meeting and playing with his grandchild. He remained Mira's pillar of strength. He still shared his wisdom through regular phone conversations.

It was time for Mira to get her education back on track. Over the years of going through storms, her academics suffered the consequences. Education was her pathway to her success. So, she turned to prayer for a breakthrough. Next, she gathered her strength, approached the Dean of the Engineering department, and presented her case.

"Dr. Ritz, I have a baby to provide for and cannot afford any more delay in life. I need to graduate and get a job. Will you allow me to condense the remaining two semesters, including the senior project proposal and presentation, into this last semester?"

The Dean approved her request. Calling her by her last name, he said: "Do not let me down."

No, the approval was not a miracle. Mira went through a lot, from risking homelessness multiple times, losing her friend Angela, flirting with darkness, grief, heartbreak, and custody battles. So, her GPA was two-something (the lower end) out of four. Her poor academic performance did not warrant the Dean's approval. She attended part-time and fell. Why would he trust her to pass when combining two full semesters? So, all things considered, there was no reason to grant her request, but God. She devoted herself to tireless efforts and stayed in the library until someone kicked her out. She got perfect scores on her senior project planning and presentation and most other courses. Her perseverance paid off; her GPA improved, and Mira graduated as a Civil Engineer in roadway infrastructure.

She called her father and shared the great news. He was very proud of her and repeated,

"You did it!"

Adding to his excitement, her family and Mira's few friends celebrated her success. The graduation was bittersweet as she missed her mother. However, Mira believed she had the VIP seat as a Special Angel.

Looking back at her life journey, Mira understood there are at least three kinds of people: Those who love you. They stay within reach. Then there are the ones who care out of convenience. They milk the cow if it produces milk, but there is no loyalty. They would turn their back on you any minute. Others will stay close to see you fall to elevate themselves.

"Such is life," Mira learned the hard way.

With her academic dream fulfilled, Mira made a bold prayer following graduation.

"God, I need 30 days of rest. After that, please grant me a good-paying job in my profession."

She had submitted one application, and God's faithfulness was great. Mira not only got the job, but it was also a perfect fulfillment of her prayer right on time. She has been working as an engineer since. She also returned to work at the college, not as a tutor, but as a Mathematics Professor. The journey took seven years to live out her academic dream, and becoming a professor was the icing on the cake. Her intellectual accomplishment felt like a burdening chip had fallen off her shoulder. She was ready to soar into her great destiny.

A Personal Vow

Mira was now an accomplished professional. However, she still wanted marriage and to have more children, one more girl and two boys. Until then, one was everything. She pledged to only introduce Stella to a prospective husband to shield her child from bonding with men who had no intention of being part of their lives. Mira knew too well the emotional toll of short-term attachments, and Stella was too precious, needing all the protection Mira could provide. She had already witnessed enough chaos in her life, amplified by the tension between her parents. Greg held a grudge against Mira for having custody. So, he seized every opportunity to pick fights, reminding her she would pay for it.

Sundays, when he picked Stella up for a few hours, Mira would brace herself for the aftermath. For instance, she might have refused to give Stella candy at home, but Greg would load Dora the Explorer's backpack with lollipops and Skittles. It was heartbreaking to see her daughter's eyes welling up with tears as Mira tried to protect her, or in that case, her teeth. Mira often wished that Greg was not in her life because of the tension that rose between them every Sunday, but she could not deny Stella the opportunity to spend time with her father. Stella deserved to have him in her life. Was it the right decision? Some days, it felt so, while others did not. This continued for 18 years. However, playing both the good and bad cop roles was Mira's most challenging aspect of single motherhood, but her love for Stella remained unquestionable.

What did Stella say about Mira's motherhood? **Story 18** gives a glimpse. On the other end, Mira attests she tried to do the right thing! Motherhood forced her to mature, fostering a sense of vigilance, carefulness, and heightened awareness of their worth. Throughout this journey, she remained steadfast in trusting God and continued to live by the values instilled by her parents, summarized in the phrase, "The fear of the Lord is the beginning of wisdom" (Proverbs 9:10). The future was bright and full of promise.

.

Story 15: Journey to the Past

Delia's Inspiring Legacy

Mira's self-help process included staying more in touch with the rest of her family back in her homeland. While every family member enriched her life, there was something unique about her sister, Delia. Do you remember her in **Story 1** when Mira would go to the river as a child and collect pebbles and shells to play with?

Delia, a year older than Mira, was born with a medical condition that confined her to a wheelchair. However, she was always cheerful and hardworking. Delia loved attending church every Sunday and singing in front of the congregation. To earn spending money, she knitted baby sweaters, socks, hats, scarves, and traded goods by hiring someone to run her errands and report back to her. Her presence could lighten up the room with laughter; her wisdom and life views humbled everyone who met her. However, her total dependency on others, her inability to procreate, watching everyone move on but her, and having to adapt to new people all the time was unbearable.

When their mother died, Delia went to live with other family members who cared for her until their father remarried. She returned to live with the stepmother. Sadly, what started as a new home took a different turn. The stepmother had her own family. Delia and anyone else who still lived there felt lost. Witnessing everything morphing from a once peaceful home filled with laughter and joy to the extreme opposite, Delia endured the change in silence. Her dad was her buffer, and the love she continued to receive was a lifeline. However, he could only be present sometimes because of his work. The long-distance love she received from those who left obstructed the complete picture of a reality she endured, from which she shielded everyone. When the family became aware, it was too late to do anything.

Since Mira came to the USA, they had stayed connected over the phone, and during their father's visits, they would exchange letters. Someone helped her to write. Their friendship continued despite the distance. One day, Mira woke up from a dream about her sister wanting to talk. Tired, she returned to sleep, planning to call her later. While asleep, the phone rang once. Mira stayed in bed. About half an hour later, it rang again. This time, she answered. Her brother greeted her. Mira was so happy, especially after revealing he was at their dad's house. He had stopped by.

"Delia wanted to talk to you," he said.

"I am sorry. I was tired and needed extra sleep, so here I am. Can I talk to her?" Mira responded.

"I am sorry, too. They rushed her to the hospital, but she wanted to talk to you first. It looks bad. Her swollen face was unrecognizable." Her brother explained.

Minutes later, a sinking feeling settled in her chest as her brother called again to let her know her beloved sister Delia had passed away. Overwhelmed with shock and guilt, Mira could not shake the weight of what had happened, haunted by the knowledge that her decision to ignore the call may have cost her the chance to say goodbye.
Top of Form

As guilt built-in, Mira noticed seeds of self-inflicted judgment taking root and stopped their growth and multiplication. She recognized self-blame was selfish. It shifted the attention away from the painful loss onto Mira. So, she uprooted it, refocused her thoughts and understood Delia had gone to rest.

She cried in silence for too long. Unable to escape the wheelchair, living with its repercussions made death liberating. She lived beyond her life expectancy. Doctors predicted she would not live past her teenage years. She overthrew their predictions and lived till a few days before turning 40. Everyone, Mira included, became better people because once upon a time, there was Delia. Despite challenges, she brought light to people's lives, a testament to a life well lived.

She rested beside their mother, and Mira always wondered what she wanted to tell her over the phone. Delia was Mira's role model. For the pain Mira endured in America, she told herself, *"If my sister Delia can do it, so can I."*

Delia embodied living through life's storms. Like their mother, she is alive in Mira's heart and countless others and will continue to be a source of inspiration. At some point, Mira would have to return home to pay respects.

Honoring Them

Mira could have stayed away since not returning home made her mother's and sister's deaths unreal. However, one can only sweep pain under the rug for so long. If not managed, it would mount into disasters. So, it was time to pay respect and face the grief that lurked undetected. There was no need to return home broken and unaccomplished. When she returned to Africa, she was a professional engineer, mathematics professor, and at peace with herself.

In addition, God blessed her beyond expectations. She was ready to pour back into the lives of others, a childhood commitment she still held at heart. It was not to rebuild roads yet. Priorities shifted. Mira considered education a right, not a privilege. So, she wanted to return to her homeland and build schools, prioritizing academic access for children living in villages. Her father would help to make it happen.

She also wanted to share great news with him and the rest of the family. After years of single motherhood, she met Jamal, and he proposed to her before Mira returned home for the first time in decades. Mira's daughter, now a teenager, loved Jamal. Her love life may have fallen short from a high-school love affair like her parents,' but who was counting? She was on top of the world and ready to be Jamal's wife, and her daughter would benefit from having a home with two loving parents, as Mira did growing up.

For years, Mira shared with her father her pain from being single. He would answer every time:

"Your time will come. Be patient and have faith."

So, Mira, now engaged, looked forward to her father walking her down the aisle. Traveling back to Africa to show him the engagement ring, the most beautiful jewelry she had ever owned, was a great segue into the upcoming wedding celebrations, which were to unfold upon her return to the USA. The time came, and she headed to the motherland. About 20 hours later, she stood before the door of her childhood home. The tiny baby plants she had planted two decades earlier had grown into trees. Those on the front porch lost their vibrancy, and some vases looked rusty. Everything felt gloomy; even the front door told on the sadness inside. The physical structure remained unchanged, but time rewrote the narrative. She knocked, turned the doorknob to the unlocked door, and walked in.

Melancholic waves filled the house, asphyxiating the familiar warmth, grace, and joy that Mira's mother once provided. It was now the stepmother's house, her rules, and her aura. The loving sound she last heard when leaving for the USA and God's presence was no longer there, which left Mira feeling estranged. Her father still sat in the same spot. But this time, he was surviving, and the meal on the table reflected his new reality. For a moment, Mira came face to face with the environment where Delia had a stroke, and sadness filled her heart, but she shook it off.

Without turning his head, her dad chuckled in a moment of fatherly instinct and said, "I saw the point of your nose and knew it was you."

Beyond the complexity of that moment, his spirit remained the same: kind, caring, and giving. He invited her to join him at the table for a meal of Fufu, two small bony fried fish, and some vegetables. The sight of the table broke Mira's heart, and she refused to eat so he would have enough, but he insisted, moving the plate to the center between them and said:

"Eat!"

They shared a modest meal. The stepmother sat on the other side of the table across from her dad, and Mira met her for the first time. Mira went with the flow for her dad, holding a small talk. She did not stay too long, as he looked exhausted. After kissing him on top of his head, as Stella, his granddaughter, did, she left, promising to return tomorrow.

"You promise, right?" He said.

"Yes, papa!" She responded, adding that she had great news to share with him.

It was true, but she also wanted to give him something to look forward to. When she walked in, he looked like someone who gave up on life. Time and adversities had taken a toll on him.

As excited as she was to see her dad, she felt a hint of resentment toward her stepmother. Their union somehow betrayed her late mother. It wasn't her father's remarrying that bothered her; instead, Mira had hoped his wife would treat him as the king of the castle he was, with royal dignity, but the reality fell short of that hope.

Bring Me Flour

The following day, they were both rested. As Mira entered the house, her father looked great and rejuvenated in his attire. He was on his way to teach Hebrew and Greek. Mira caught him right in time to reveal the surprise—her diamond engagement ring.

He paused, took a moment of silence, and requested flour from his wife, standing in the doorway to the kitchen. When she brought a small bowl, he specified,

"Not this kind. Bring me the white one," a gesture steeped in tradition.

People would spread white flour or powder on the person to celebrate special occasions, and Mira's engagement was long overdue, according to Mira! He grabbed a handful and spread it on her left hand, danced, sang, and ended the celebration with prayer. Mira's heart warmed. She imagined her mother and sister celebrating in heaven as well.

As the celebration continued, her dad reminded her,

"Didn't I tell you not to worry about marriage, and your day will come?" He said with such calm, holding back his tears of joy.

"You said that, papa," Mira replied, finding herself in the middle of her dream come true and rejoicing with her father.

He made his way to the university, and Mira left with her sister to go to the gravesite and pay respect to her mother and sister. It was an emotionally charged day. She cried. As tears ran down her face in disbelief, the temporary nature of life humbled her to appreciate the value of leaving a positive legacy. She replayed the selfish decisions of hiding, taken out of anxiety, and it broke her heart at the missed opportunities. Their graves became a constant reminder of how invaluable breath is and why we should not take life for granted. With both her mother and sister, a missed phone call became the last attempt to communicate.

Seeing their names on the tombstones led her to imagine what lay beneath, and her already fragile heart broke all over again. Then, she felt a gentle breeze, and a sense of peace filled her heart as if her mother and sister had affirmed that they were okay.

"I guess cemeteries are not that frightening when they host the remains of your loved one," Mira concluded.

They walked away, heading back to the car, more aware of how little control she had in life and more ready than ever to live a meaningful life.

Later that day, Mira and her dad immersed themselves in the school initiative. The goal was for Mira to return to America, do fundraising, and return in December to finalize the school plan with him.

The Ancestor Fall

It was an honor for Mira to be answered to prayers for children, their parents, and the Chief living in the village where they planned to build the school. God blessed her financially, and with the support of her father, family, and friends, she was ready to give back. Amidst the commitment to serve, there lingered a tinge of sadness. Three decades had passed since Mira played with some children in that village. It is also where her father spent part of his childhood. Yet, new generations still grappled with the persistent challenge of illiteracy. As such, she committed to formal education empowerment as a ladder to climb out of poverty into a world of opportunities.

Mira had to return to the US to finish planning and would return to the DRC to build the school. In the meantime, she began school registration and had children learn from an abandoned building, starting with the first grade. On day 1, there were a handful of children. Soon enough, hundreds of children were off the street and into classrooms. It was a celebration for everyone, especially the children.

Looking ahead, she planned the next trip in six months to continue schoolwork. While celebrating Thanksgiving in the US, the phone rang, and once again, it flipped everything upside down, crashing hope and dream. Her dad collapsed in the same living room where she last saw him. They took him to the local clinic where his late wife once worked as a midwife and then transported him to a larger hospital, mirroring what happened with Mira's mom.

At some point, he mumbled a few things, trying to explain what happened between him and Mira's stepmother, but could only say a few words. Then, he asked to remove his watch, and after reciting "The Lord's Prayer" in Hebrew, he said,

"I am ready."

When they rushed him to the hospital, he had already made his reverence to life and embraced death. Not even the heartfelt weeping of his children could get him to change his mind. Mira believed God gave him a glimpse of heaven and the choice to stay alive. But looking at where he would return after replaying what happened when he collapsed, as well as coming back paralyzed from a stroke, letting go was liberating.

He deserved a dignified reverence. He tried to say something to Mira, but his voice was too weak to come through the phone. He had a stroke. That was the end of this brave man who gave the best of himself to the world. He left grown orphans, but no one raised in a loving home is too grown to live without parental love. So, the loss caused deep wounds.

Mira was not just returning to build the school and show the ring. She wanted to get to know her father beyond just being a dad. Who was this young boy who sold vegetables and became a global leader? He changed lives, inspiring a sense of self-agency, honor, and autonomy. This man knew how to touch souls in the best ways. She will never get the answers. There would be bits and pieces, but it would always be incomplete and different had he told his story.

> *"I guess death forces us all to live with voids, and such is life,"* Mira concluded.

Then, Mira returned to bury him, and thousands of people came to honor the man who had touched countless hearts, setting high life standards for everyone who knew him. Later, Mira learned he knew he would not live long enough for their appointment. He died within thirty days of the appointment.

Mira continued with the school project with other supporters, and living life to the fullest became an act of preserving and cherishing the memories of those who shaped her success. If those who die in Christ get to see each other, he went to be with his high school sweetheart, his daughter, and many loved ones in dignity. He was a mastermind; his work ethic, visions, and life views spoke volumes, leaving a permanent legacy. "Ancestor" was one of the many nicknames people gave him. He was fearless, a living legend, and a well of knowledge and wisdom. As for Mira's future wedding, she would have to find someone else to walk her down the aisle. Neither of her parents could make it.

PART 6: MIRA FACES MIRA

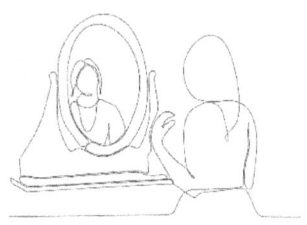

"You are 1st, in the middle, and last all at the same time. It all depends on where you place yourself. So, just put your best foot forward; the world has already decided who to think of you." - *Hadassah/Mulowa*

- Story 16: The Ironic Poetry
- Story 17: Rising Through Brokenness
- Story 18: Awakened Warrior

Story 16: The Ironic Poetry

Down The Aisle

One year after her father's death, Jamal gave a dowry as a symbolic gesture to honor Mira's parents and solidify his intention to marry her. Mira's dad designated a family member in the USA as their representative. When he made the plan, he did not expect death would cause their absence. It was a matter of convenience and logic.

A year and a half later, she walked down the aisle. Photographers captured precious moments as the bride prepared for her wedding, surrounded by loved ones in an ancient castle. Her champagne-colored short-sleeved dress stretched on the bed, adorned with sparkling intricate details. The ring bearers, the flower girl's laughter, and Mira's loved ones surrounded Mira. She was on top of the world. Her imagination ran into the future, similar to the experience when they went hiking at the mountain, and she would surrender to her destiny. The only difference this time was that she was living her marriage aspiration dream. In a few hours, she would be Jamal's wife. It was one of the best days of her life.

The photographer continued to capture breathtaking memories as they made their way to the car, ready to take the soon-to-be bride to the Church. Then, they reached the Church. Mira emanated grace, and her eyes mirrored the richness of the moment. The elegant and flawless groom stood at the altar with his groomsmen chosen for their long-standing bonds. Mira's bridesmaids, dressed in African fabric outfits she designed, were beautiful queens.

Stella, her daughter, was the maid of honor. Mira thought of it as the perfect gift for her 18th birthday. The bride herself designed the bridesmaids' outfits and made Stella's and Stella's friend. The flower girl and ring bearers were perfect angels. The guests at the Church represented a blend of rich cultural backgrounds, symbolizing sisterhood, friendship, diversity, and unity.

There was a pinch of sadness, Mira's deceased parents. Her sister Delia was also gone. But she could not attend the wedding even if she were still alive. Doctors forbid it since she could not handle airplane altitudes. However, other family members represented them well, and Mira found comfort in knowing Heaven hosted them. So, they had VIP access at the wedding.

Pastor gestured for the audience to stand up. Next, the African beat dropped; the Church's two doors swung open. Mira walked down the aisle accompanied by her sister. It was bittersweet since she hoped her father would give her away but was grateful; he lived long enough to celebrate their engagement, and her sister fit well in his shoes. When Jamal and Mira's eyes met, he teared up for the first time. Time froze, capturing perfection.

Once at the altar, they exchanged vows before God and the crowd. She fulfilled her marriage aspiration, entering a new phase of life as a wife, which set the stage for their beautiful journey ahead.

In front of their loved ones, Jamal and Mira committed to their promises to build each other up. Anchored in the scripture from Genesis 1:1, their union echoed God's work of giving people access to Heaven on earth through their gifts of wisdom. They were both blessed with the ability to touch hearts with words and pledged to serve. After their "I Do," the crowd cheered and applauded with God as their witness.

Let's Dance

Guests headed to the reception hall. The bride and groom eternalized more precious moments outside the Church with the photographer before joining their guests. The room was lit with candlelight. Mira's cousin helped decorate the hall. Mira and her daughter crafted the centerpiece for each table. So, it was a collective effort to turn the hall into a breathtaking masterpiece.

The guests filled the room, creating a perfect cultural blend of Africa and America. The DJ played African songs, R&B, and gospel music, enhancing the night's beauty. The ambiance was surreal. Guests from other receptions in the mansion could not help but peep in. The wedding was fit for royalty. Mira was ushered into a great destiny and felt beyond blessed! She was ready to step into the world as a power couple.

The excitement continued as Jamal reserved a surprise for his wife. She often pleaded with him to dance during their courtship, but he would refuse. Instead, he would tease her, hinting at his talents. On their wedding night, he unleashed his mastery of the art, spinning and floating with each move, narrating his love for her. He danced, owning the floor, captivating everyone, and Mira fell in love again.

There was one more surprise. Soft and heartfelt guitar strumming, and an angelic voice filled the room. Mira's eyes lit up, and her face broke into a radiant smile. Her daughter dedicated a performance to her "Mommy." Mira, in awe, cried tears of joy, love, and gratitude. Her daughter, a beautiful person inside and out, was all grown, and life came full circle. She was almost fifty when her aspiration for marriage came to fruition.

She raised Stella as a single parent. So, through marriage, she planned to create a home where love would be the only spoken language in their union. Together, they would provide a loving two-parent home so her daughter could benefit from such relational wealth as Mira did, watching her parents. It was time to create more positive legacies together as one.

The Paradox of The Altar

Let us revisit the start of this lifelong dream of marriage. Reflecting on Jamal and Mira's journey together while dating, they were perfect for each other and spoke for long hours, with each conversation gaining deeper meaning. There was never a dull moment; they were like two fitting puzzle pieces. Jamal once told Mira he had never met someone like her, who, within less than two minutes of conversation, read him and saw his pain.

Mira also fell in love with his depth. She had met no one who could reach her as he did. Together, they were like a mirror reflecting each other's excellence. Jamal and Mira were the compass pointing in all the right directions. Their relationship was like an infinite looped maze, with every turn leading to intriguing treasure hunts. Everybody in her family and her few friends knew she was in love. And to top it off, Mira's daughter trusted him. In the end, the wedding sealed everything.

Eight months later, he filed for divorce, accusing her of being unfaithful over a hug he witnessed at a reception. Mira was not perfect, but the man she married was everything to her, and when she became his wife, it was a title and role she intended to honor. It was the missing piece of her life. She could not soil it as nothing in this world was enticing enough for her to gamble her marriage cheating.

It took her over two decades from when she came to America and approaching 50 to walk down the aisle. Multiple prospects wanted to marry her. But Jamal was the one, even if it cost her giving up to have more children. He had his own and did not want anymore. That was ok, Mira had Stella.

She never cheated on him. So, as her mind spun in multiple directions, trying to make sense of everything, her heart bled to the sword of the breakup. She invested a lot in loving Jamal. He may claim the same. But watching the fabric of the unfinished world she wanted to build crumble under the weight of her shattered marriage was devastating. It was a free fall into a ruthless void of despair. Hope disappeared, swallowed by life's malicious rhythms that delighted in tormenting her. Each creak of the floorboards in her house whispered her anguish. The promises carved in her heart to love her even more after the wedding became keloids of shame. The days blurred together in a haze of tear-stained nights and sleepless dawns, whispering,

"You are a loser. Can't even hold on to a man?"

Mira's once resilient spirit was now faltering under the weight of personal grief. All of her eggs were in one basket, and her destiny crashed. Her reflection in the mirror testified to the agony etched upon her face. Eyes, once gleaming with hope, now drowned in doubt, haunted by an unfulfilled future.

Then Jamal gave her hope to start over.

Dark Path

He offered to schedule marriage counseling appointments. Naïve, she believed they could work it out. Sadly, the sessions became a painful spectacle, a boxing ring where they could bruise and break each other with words while the therapist watched, captivated by Jamal's charm. Weeks spent on the therapist's couch exposed voids that echoed the mournful rhythms of a dead relationship going back to pre-marriage. Mira was losing her mind and life's meaning. One day, the therapist called her to say,

> "Just tell him you cheated and change the narrative so you can fix your marriage. Jamal loves you. He is just hurt."

Standing under a bridge, Mira, ready to walk into the office, froze. She could feel a monster taking over, whispering dark thoughts. Her heart palpitating, she leaned against her vehicle, and the darkness said,

> *"Get in the car and go deal with her,"* but a softer voice replied,

"That isn't me talking to you. You will regret every decision you make if you act on your rage. Go into the office."

The marriage counseling was more toxic and crippling. Mira listened to her conscience and stopped collecting prescribed scars. 'Therapy' ended. Yet, when he came to take his things - the car, the engagement ring, and a couple of shirts hanging in her closet - Mira felt new levels of pain. Those moments unveiled even more venom, and her heart would break again.

> *"Did he love me, or did he go with my flow, which I made affordable for him?"* These paralyzing thoughts snowballed into:

> *"You are stupid. Jamal showed you repeatedly where his heart was, NOT WITH YOU! He proposed to hold you captive because you were returning to your country. Marrying you was not in his mind. How many times did he break up with you? You should have stayed away but were too desperate for marriage, and your love for him blinded you. It was your downfall, and you brought this on yourself. You could have avoided the divorce had you accepted his heart was elsewhere."*

Shamed, humiliated, angry, and afraid, she watched herself spiral downhill into a suffocating hollow of resentment and revenge. Then, her bruised ego kicked in, urging her to stand up for herself, not in the best way. Invaded by darkness and at the peak of her pain, she hoped he suffered, and such feelings brought relief. Venom continued to rise within, encouraging her to feed the growing monster. Pinned on the path of vindictiveness, she knew what awaited beyond those opened emotional doors was not only irreversible, but they led her straight to a mental institution, prison, and even a grave. She could not act on her thoughts.

Echoes of Emptiness

Jamal broke her heart. She needed a path away from the tension between good and evil that tore her apart. She turned to sleeping pills and alcohol, but that brought only short-lived relief. Once sober, shadows on her bedroom walls danced at the beat of migraine, reflecting the chaos within her mind. The moon's glow cast a ghostly light on her face, mirroring the emptiness she felt. By then, her daughter had graduated from Community College and moved to campus to further her education. So, Mira was alone and unaware of who she had become. Her once lively space transformed into a battleground, where every day became a struggle against the intruding darkness. Even the once cheerful sounds of birds outside her bedroom window became painful reminders of the empty nest.

Mira became a lifeless shell of herself. As seeds of self-deterioration grew, they filled the void in her heart. She felt trapped in cycles of pain, anguish, and negative self-talk, which birthed low self-esteem. As it spread, she became paralyzed and rotted from within, begging for relief, and found none. She could not help but notice some people celebrating her descent into hell. As pressure increased each day, the roots of her emotional turmoil deepened. Mira felt lost.

Divorce was the darkest battle she had ever faced. To restore a sense of normalcy, Mira contemplated begging Jamal to withdraw the divorce paper to hold on to the wife's title. It would not have been for love since he was already gone. But she knew better than staying married to only tally years of marriage. It would have killed her. The thought of Jamal standing at her gravesite as the broken widow and offering a heartfelt obituary was a satisfaction she refused to give to the universe. These thoughts became why she did not give up on herself and assembled the shattered pieces of her heart and mind. With this mindset and knowing some people loved her, she forged forward.

Story 17: Rising Through Brokenness

Redeeming Journey

"If I could love who I am, there is no need to kill me to become." Mira told herself as she fought the internal battles that had spun out of control. In searching for answers from within, she landed on these questions:

1. Why did he marry me? There was more than enough time during our engagement of over two and a half years to break up.
2. Why did he invest in the wedding and promise the world in front of everyone just to pull the rug from under my feet?
3. Was the marriage just an illusion, a failed magic trick?
4. Did I sacrifice myself in pursuit of an idealized marriage?
5. How did I allow myself to get here?

To answer, she tried pushing through the heavy clouds hanging over her spirit, but her wings were too weak. Staying down under the debris of her brokenness became too suffocating. The debilitating choruses of words such as *"You are a terrible mother. Cannot even build a home,"* name-calling, past traumas, and those resulting from feeling like a failure were hard to silence. She traced her brokenness back to high school. It came down to this harsh reality. Mira did not know her worth when entering relationships. So, she set herself up to collect emotional scars. She kept adapting to the demand of the relations, digging pits of self-sabotage, and found herself in too deep.

This self-awareness made her feel like a fraud.

Through it all, only one person bore witness to the depth of her trauma and despair—let us call her Aloe. She journeyed with Mira to figure her way out of the confusing life maze and through the prison walls of her mind. Aloe called to check on her, prayed for her, and said she would bring food and even drop by unannounced.

One night, she had another episode of negative self-talk and self-punishment, but there was no one to fight. She turned herself into a punching bag. Then she had an epiphany:

"If something in me is still breakable, then something is still intact."

This shift in perspective inspired a desire to preserve what remained unbroken in her. She summoned the strength to pick herself up. This was a whole new process of its own. One rainy night, amid lightning and thunder, she collapsed to her knees to pray, haunted by unanswered questions. As her chest tightened under the weight of her pain and fears, she reached out to the God she feared and yelled,

"God, let your will be done. I surrender all to you. I do not know what it means but take away what is killing me. You asked me to pick up my cross and follow you. It is now too heavy to bear, and I am tired. Help me!"

Hours later, she rose from the ground, ready to evict victimhood born from the outfall of the divorce and past life traumas. Pilling off emotional scabs and revisiting old wounds unraveled new layers of uncertainties. The issue was not looking back. It was the new lyrics from choruses of past dark melodies that created new fears. They played:

> *"You are 50. It is too late to start over. Your daughter moved out to college; incompetence is your legacy for her, and she is lucky to be away from you. Now, you are too old to be at square one; go work it out with Jamal; at least you won't age alone."*

Then, God changed the narrative of these harmful and derogatory thoughts. She understood Stella flying out of the nest was part of her daughter's becoming, and children needed to spread their wings to build their own nest. Yes, Mira was almost 50 then, but a sign of life has always been the heartbeat and an alive brain, not age. It became clear that had she stayed married, it would have been sleeping on a dormant volcano, similar to the relationship with Greg.

The divorce storms were still ravaging, but they became less threatening. This rebirth was frightening, as she realized marriage was an idol by which she defined her worth, and she had turned Jamal into a god. Their relationship would have worked only if she continued worshiping him. But would have been counterintuitive to her self-worth journey. So, she nurtured anything that ignited a flicker of determination within her soul to find internal peace. It was challenging, and she fumbled along the way. But, as resentment toward Jamal dissipated, Mira's healing became manageable and believable.

It was up to her to let go of the burden she asked God to carry; He was ready to intervene if Mira would stop interfering. With each tear that continued to fall, figuring out how to jump off the tormenting mental, emotional, and psychological rollercoaster ride was draining. A spark ignited a fire within her, fueling a quiet resolve to rise above brokenness.

> *"If I breathed under the emotional debris, I could rise from my crisis,"* she murmured as she mustered her resilience and reclaimed her warrior authority.

This process was also part of carrying her cross, but surrendering her burden to God in prayer allowed Him to step in and remove the life-draining sting of trials. With renewed strength to push through, Mira was on her way out of the wilderness.

Unveiling Meaning through Decluttering

A gentle internal whisper compelled her to clean, and she embarked on a mission to find meaning through decluttering. She attributed the voice to the

Holy Spirt, who led her to start in the closet. While cleaning, she sifted through old boxes and stumbled upon notes detailing her aspirations to bring happiness in people's lives. These notes went decades earlier. One note described their breakup before he even proposed to her, mirroring the reality of the divorce. God had been warning Mira all along against walking down the aisle. But Mira was blind in love.

Her heart knotted at the details of the written messages, and confronting the reality that she had stayed in the relationship and got married based on promises made her feel like a fool. She looked for someone to blame, but the mirror reflected her image, reminding her she pulled Jamal into her dream and even held on to the relationship. Postponing everything was his way of showing his stand, but Mira tolerated delays. So, he offered more of it. He was polite but not committed to their destiny. These realizations shook Mira to the core, but she was steadfast in her determination to reach the other side of the breakthroughs.

One stormy night, as she went through boxes covered in spider webs, the rain poured, lightning struck, and thunder shook the heavens. For a moment, she thought the storm was a metaphor for her life and the universe was mocking her. Covered in tears as she unveiled years of missed teachable moments, Mira soon realized she was under God's grace.

As in Psalm 77:18, thunder and lightning were indeed metaphors, but nothing was mocking about them. They were God's strength and authority, calling Mira to regain composure and reminding her to keep walking in the split sea toward the promised land. The rain reminded her it had collected her tears, which she would use to nurture her transformation and growth, turning the pit where she was buried into wells.

Mira committed to pushing through and giving birth to a better version of herself. Labor was hard, but she embraced morphing into her calling for excellence. This self-belief disrupted victimhood, and she stood tall and unapologetic. It took a few life bruises to see it, but mercy and grace disallowed the brokenness she endured to corrupt the goodness within her. This preserved virtue allowed God to locate her amid life's storms.

With God on her side, Mira was on the brink of freedom, where countless great possibilities awaited. The self-inflicted shackles were loose; she allowed herself to walk out of self-imprisonment to meet the world and many people who loved and were looking/waiting for her healing. Decluttering was the best path out of the dark pit, not just for her closet but, most importantly, for her mind, heart, and relationship with her daughter.

While in the pit of life adversities, she built silos of personal grief. They created a barrier between mother and child. Stella was going through a lot, and Mira was unaware. Sadly, she passed on to her child the harmful tendency of silent suffering and isolation. So, her rebirth also meant getting the train back on track to repair and strengthen their damaged relationship. Divorce was painful. The threat of losing Stella was frightening. So, she knew where to surrender her pain and fears to God. She did just that!

The Mirror

Mira ran away and isolated herself whenever life became difficult. However, this time, she realized she had to stay away from the walls of self-imprisonment. Her life connected to others, such as those who walked into the fire to pull her or put it out. Her life was also for those waiting for her healing to heal. Mira needed to confront her reality. So, she gazed into the mirror. The reflection was a worn-out shadow of herself. She took a harder look. It revealed years of poor decisions, relational stress, anxiety, depression, and trauma that had caught up to her.

Rather than seeking help, she learned to conceal pain behind facades of normalcy. Pretending turned out to be even more draining. She continued facing the mirror. It showed her as a beggar of validation of self-worth. The constant need for external affirmation made her compromise her values to fit in. As she adjusted her life to meet other people's expectations, it spiraled downhill into self-sabotage, and she did not know how to push the brake to stop. So, she tried to find comfort in the ride and subscribed to the misconception that love conquered any obstacle, neglecting to address issues head-on.

She had made progress in her healing journey, but standing in front of the mirror revealed more work to do. To pierce through the remaining obstacles and bring Mira home to the 'fearfully and wonderfully' made Mira, she committed to see her healing through.

Story 18: Embracing the Inner Warrior

"Every time we stand to fight for something, we have already won. So, let's carry the fight to the end to see the results. Stand up for yourself, soldiers!"

Awaken Mira's Inner Warrior

Mira's healing journey was tumultuous. There were patterns to break, which was the pivotal point to anchor her healing. Here is a glimpse into it.

For years, Mira drifted through the currents of her relationships, never realizing her own agency within them. But one day, she realized she was not meant to drift with the flow; she was the flow itself. She could navigate obstacles, forge her path, and redefine her journey. This self-awareness changed everything.

As she looked back on her breakups and hardships, Mira saw them not as setbacks but as blessings in disguise. Each bruise and stumble had tempered her spirit and shaped her into the person she was becoming. She understood that stagnation was not the end of the road but a detour on the way to growth.

Yet, even as she embraced this newfound perspective, life continued to test her resolve. Adversities piled up, threatening to overwhelm her at every turn. There were moments when she wanted to give up, when prayers seemed to fall on deaf ears. But she discovered a reservoir of strength she never knew existed within her. In that moment, Mira faced a choice: to remain broken and at the mercy of circumstances or to embark on a journey of self-discovery and healing. With faith as her guide, she chose the latter, committing herself to rebirth and renewal.

As she walked that path, Mira realized that one of her biggest mistakes had been neglecting herself in pursuit of love. She had sacrificed her own well-being for validation from others. But like the ocean that never asks the riverbed to support it, Mira vowed never to allow anyone else to dictate her worth. For as far as her memory led her back, she was an ocean trying to fit in a sink, and she did not know it, and this limiting belief made her brokenness attractive. Then God's grace and mercy found her and opened her eyes to exploring her best version instead.

She understood that true empowerment meant no longer seeking permission to be herself. It meant reclaiming her authority and refusing to settle for anything less than she deserved. Armed with this newfound sense of self, Mira embraced life with zeal. Gone were the days of surviving; now, Mira was determined to live. She refused to waste another moment wondering what could have been or testing the waters of uncertainty. She understood that life was too precious to be squandered on regrets.

And though the journey from victimhood to empowerment was far from easy, Mira knew it was worth it. In realizing the doors that had led to her own deterioration, she had unlocked the key to her healing. And with each step forward, she grew bold, more truly herself. Mira found Mira.

Hidden Gems in Scars

As Mira approached the last leg of her healing journey, it was essential to face the scars of her past. They were a testament to the battles fought and the strength within. With a newfound sense of self-love, she revisited the old wounds, viewing them not as sources of pain but as markers of her growth and triumphs.

Reflecting on her past, Mira would hide behind facades, afraid to show her true self for fear of judgment. She had the gift of finding solutions, but most of her surroundings took it as' pride.' So, she would go with the flow to avoid friction and tension until it became frustrating to remain silent, smile to take the blow and watch the hitter walk away in victory. But, through her healing process, she understood these facades served a purpose. They projected confidence in facing adversities, turning past scars into symbols of tenacity, not weakness.

She took steps further back to trace the origins of her pain. It was in high school when she was ridiculed for bleeding on her skirt, then the attempted sexual assaults. Fast forwarding to America, a series of occurrences stripped her of strength and desire to stand up for herself. It was not anybody's fault. Nobody forced her into any relationship. She set the tone for her treatment and even made herself prey. Unfortunately, she could take none of it back. But God is faithful. He extended her grace and mercy to reveal she had been powerful all along. Her tomboy personality, once seen as a liability, was a source of strength. It was ok to stand firm and tall even if it made others uncomfortable. This self-assurance made it possible to be unapologetic.

All her wounds and the resulting scars sprang from love and loving. There was nothing wrong with it, except she sought validation. Now that her eyes opened, she vowed to keep loving without compromising her worth. It was ok to be vulnerable, but only in safe environments. The term 'safe' meant exposing her vulnerability only to those intending to help her pick herself up and grow from her mistakes or challenges.

In her healing journey, Mira discovered that true peace only came from sincere prayer, faith, and patience. Though there were moments of doubt and unanswered prayers, she recognized God was always by her side, guiding her through the storms of life. With each scar etched onto her skin or lingering in her heart, Mira gained emotional and psychological fortitude to be kind to herself. The wounds were not symbols of pain but of triumph.

Equipped with self-awareness, Mira embraced her rebirth. As she stood at the threshold of her genesis, ready to live, she had one more obstacle to face—herself.

Ushered Into Fullness

Mira's journey toward finding Mira shifted with one more moment of divine intervention orchestrated by none other than her own daughter, Stella. It was miraculous! Not even in her wildest dream, could she have guessed the child she gave birth would hasher her into fullness, handing Mira the last piece of her healing.

Mom went to visit her daughter at the university. Stella shared adventures and news of a student's life and showcased her decorations and art pieces. One was Mira's on a small canvas, and she could not see it until finished. They then discussed classes. The moment was refreshing, and they found comfort in the familiar rhythm of their conversations.

Next, her daughter asked: "How are you doing, Mommy?"

Mira almost choked as her throat knotted, trying to hold back her tears. Beneath the surface, Mira carried a burden of pain, self-doubt, and low self-esteem stemming from the wounds of divorce and shattered dreams. So, she poured out her heart to her daughter sitting on the bed and Mira on a beanbag, admitting she was tired of being strong as the weight of failure tore her soul.

"I hate going home; the silence echoes—you failed. At almost 50, you will never get married again. Look at the example you set for your daughter. Your parents inspired you. What is your legacy to Stella?"

With each word spoken, Mira felt the weight of her insecurities bearing down on her, replying in her head to the cruel names she had been called in the past. Then she took a deep breath and concluded her rundown with,

"I am tired of taking three steps forward and nine steps back."

But then Stella interjected with the gift that silenced all the internal storms and anchored Mira's healing into self-acceptance. This is how the story unfolded!

"Mommy, can I say something? Hey, Mommy, let me tell you a story!" With anticipation, Mira responded,

"Yes, go ahead, Love!" ready to receive her daughter's wisdom.

"Let me tell you a story about someone incredible," Stella said and continued.

"I know a person who landed in a new country without knowing the language, yet against all odds, became a successful engineer and math professor. And that's not all—she tackled the challenges of raising a fantastic child as a single mother. She founded a non-profit to give back to her home country and built a school to support underprivileged kids in Africa. Plus, she is writing books that are going to help many people. She is a great Mathematics Professor, and her students love her. Right now, she is doing her master's in psychology. Guess what? All my friends love her; she is among the kindest people I know. Would you like to meet her? Mommy, MOMMY, MOMMY!!! THE PERSON YOU ARE TRYING TO BECOME IS YOU! Can I curse? I will pay you a dollar?"

We did not allow cursing at home. It came with penalties.

"Sure, only this one time," Mira replied.

"You are a badass!" her daughter exclaimed.

As Mira processed the story, the remaining stronghold of negative self-perception eased. A wave of peace and happiness rose inside her, and she could not help but shed tears of relief and self-awareness. It has been decades since Mira could breathe. Years of life's beating made Mira forget the tomboy who enjoyed hunting with her brother and cousins and the fearless young girl who knew how to defend herself. Yes, the struggles were real, but so was her spirit, a chamber of hope.

Only God could arrange for her daughter to hand her the missing piece to her self-liberation. If she had taken Greg and Jamal's criticisms of her motherhood to heart, her connection with Stella would have been tainted, and Mira would have been stuck in uncertainty. When Mira looked back, the relationship with her child was often under attack. It made sense because Stella held the last piece of the puzzle to Mira's walking away from self-imprisonment. Indeed, true love conquers it all in the end, and God knew self-love could only be delivered to Mira by none but her daughter for Mira to birth Mira into her magnificence.

She still aspires to get married and even adopt. Giving birth is no longer possible unless God says otherwise. Now, she is busy honoring her heartbeat with self-care, living (on purpose), working, giving back, building legacies, and loving. She knows her worth and would not trade it for anything. In the end, Mira did not look like what she went through, and getting out of the pit in the wilderness was a miracle.

CONCLUSION

Mira's dad used to say two cheeks remained safe from burns. He would explain how our cheeks function together to cool down or spit out hot food while we eat. This principle assimilated Mira's experiences. Many people were her pillars as she went through life's rollercoaster rides. Through their prayers, compassion, and unity, they were vessels of divine presence.

Her journey of becoming started as a leap of faith. She prayed to study abroad and believed formal education was the key to her life's purpose, and it was. Success was inevitable. She had a firm foundation, her parents, and their gift of faith in God. Brokenness was not part of the anticipation when she left Africa and ended up in America. In the end, Mira understood she was a shattered masterpiece. Each fragment of her troubled past was integral to her transformation. Trials made her unstoppable. Philippians 4:13 calls her capable of great things through Him who strengthened her. The Spirit God gave her does not make her timid but gives her power, love, and self-discipline, 2 Timothy 1:7.

Finding self-love helped her discover her self-worth. But the healing of her wounded soul came from trusting in the redeeming blood of Jesus Christ. She tried numbing pain in different ways, but only to collect more scars. Surrendering to God is what led her through the wilderness. Her faith flickered when the life storms became too ravaging, but she held on while wrestling with God. While clinging to her Savior, she realized the temporary fix only deepened the wounds of a bleeding heart or troubled mind. True healing comes from within, and Jesus Christ is the most affordable option. He revealed the ugly truth about her role in the mess she found herself, yet there was no judgment. Equipped with only faith and sincere prayers, she broke free, and there are no records, bills, or creditors after her.

The journey of Mira finding Mira was challenging. But she found herself on the right side of her breakthrough. In her quest to become, she did not find sustainable solace in people. She found it within. Was it too expensive? It felt that way while going through it. But in the end, her heartbeat was the most precious currency that afforded her to bounce back and soar. Mira made peace with herself, understanding she is yesterday's memory, today's gift, and tomorrow is an enigma. It is up to God to make it a present. Her only assignment was to live life to the fullest.

THE END

HEAL & BLOOM

A Life Simple Self-Help Tool to Thrive

Photo by Patrick C., 2024

"You take yourself with you everywhere you go. So, take care of yourself! You are the only one there is, a one in billions—a rare masterpiece, even if shattered!"

Hadassah/Mulowa

Dear Reader,

This guide is for anyone seeking a path forward from life adversities. It has helpful lessons and practical tips to help you find balance, especially by taking care of yourself. Although the guide is useful on its own, I recommend reading the book first. It tells Mira's story, from a playful child in Africa to struggling in America and then finding herself again. Use the offered support and advice to handle life's challenges easier. And do not forget, taking care of yourself is not selfish. So, do it!

Hadassah/ Mulowa

Introduction

Self-agency is your responsibility. With that in mind, focus on your current challenges. Who affects your life and in what ways? As you ponder this question, look at everything that makes up your world. If you rearranged your life, how different would it be? Take a moment to reflect on it! Now, imagine your life as a book. Who contributes punctuation, sentences, paragraphs, and even entire sections? What do their contributions show to or of you? If you rewrite your life narrative to fit in, whatever 'IN' is, others may have too much power over your story/reality. That is not okay. People in your life should build you up, inspire you to thrive, and discourage over-reliance.

So, as you read this guide, find any imbalances in your life, and commit to improving your narrative. Take constructive actions to achieve inner peace. You need to build a mental and emotional fortitude to regain control of your life, and remember, breaking negative tendencies, behaviors, choices, and actions could be a lonely journey. The good news is that every time self-care comes first, you advocate for yourself and create new patterns that will guide you to stop surviving and start living.

Now is the time! Advocate for your welfare and allow this *Heal and Bloom: A Life Simple Self-Help Tool* to help you on your path to revival!

The following sections include:

- Definitions
- Key Lessons
- Practical Food for Thought
- Conclusion

Definitions

Let us define 'Healing' and 'Blooming' in this guide.

Healing is to acknowledge and release emotional and mental wounds holding you back in various aspects of your life. It is to recognize past hurts, let them go, and move forward with renewed strength and clarity. Healing does not mean forgetting; it means removing the harmful sting out of life's adversities.

Blooming is to nurture yourself. This includes to set meaningful goals, observe yourself flourishing, and thrive in various aspects of your life. You will know it happened when you cannot contain your magnificence. Something inside of you shifts and the transformation is addictive. You will allow no one to tamper with it. To achieve this, you must first desire, claim, and invest in it.

Give yourself permission to heal and bloom. This is the first step towards your great destiny. Do not let anyone lie to you. It is a commitment and at times, you would want to give up. That is ok, just do not do it and pick yourself back up regardless of how many times you find yourself down. The question is, do you want it?

This guide contains 'Key Lessons,' including Three Healing Lessons and Five Blooming Lessons. It concludes with 'Practical Food for Thought.'

Key Lessons

Will you dedicate your time to self-improvement and find meaning in the insights offered here? Trust me, developing self-agency is one of the best gifts you can give yourself if you answer yes. Let these lessons grow in your heart and mind like seeds in fertile soil. Before long, you will see the positive outcomes of having peace of mind, joy, and clarity. Make yourself a priority and invest in your own development. You can start with engaging in the content of this guide, then committing to learning from your experiences. The life balance you will gain, overcoming and conquering the challenges you face, is indescribable. It could be as close as walking on water.

3 Healing Key Lessons

Confront Pains and Fears Head-On: Pain and fears often arise from anxiety. Do not ignore them. Take a journey within yourself to learn more about your true nature. In time, you will come to understand that you are stronger than you believe. If you need support, seek guidance from friends, family, or a therapist.

Seek Guidance: Seek guidance to navigate life twists and turns surrounding yourself with individuals who uphold your values and offer impartial help. You will benefit the most from their support if you invest in getting to know yourself first. Knowing yourself is essential for making informed choices and shaping your future. Guard yourself against those who prey on your insecurities. Seize control of your life and guide it towards your own greatness.

Love the Person You See in the Mirror: Accept yourself, flaws, and all, to foster stronger connections with yourself and others. You can start with self-kindness and self-compassion. If you can be ok with yourself, it makes it easier to care for someone else. Since we do not live in silos, interaction with others is inevitable. So, take care of you and remember, self-love is not selfish. It is the key to setting the right tone for your connections.

Blooming Key Lessons

Grow from Adversities: Life will throw curveballs at you, but challenges are opportunities in disguise. Confront them with bravery to thrive. Put your mind and heart to work for you. When you overcome and conquer obstacles, you build emotional and mental fortitude. So, unlike in the past, when you were vulnerable, any wind could shake you, growing from adversities deepens your roots. It becomes challenging or impossible to break you because you know your worth. Each challenge you overcome and conquer helps you stand tall. The personal victories will make committing to self-care more manageable. So, let go of what you know you are holding on and give yourself a chance to reach new heights!

Challenge Societal Expectations: Societal expectations can suffocate, but you do not have to conform. Embrace your vulnerabilities, flaws, and imperfections. Free yourself from needing external validation and cultivate genuine connections with yourself and others based on mutual respect. Stay true to yourself and strive to live your best version. What is your best version? It is the one that helps you sleep at night. Regardless of what society does, you are in misalignment if your actions get you to toss and turn. Your best version wants to thrive. Anchor it in self-care to become unshakable.

Remember, goodness never goes out of style. So, be good to yourself and manage societal expectations. If you must become, then you never were. So, stay true to yourself to avoid recreating yourself, and society will not hold you hostage because you know your worth. You can shape your inner world while the surrounding world does its thing! You build self-reliance and independence by steering your life according to your rules. Start taking charge of your life and choose positive influences, and soon you will see the results of living on your own terms.

Choose Good Over Evil: The world needs more positivity. Be positive. It improves your well-being. When you show up grounded and with purpose, your positive mindset creates powerful ripple effects that change you and others for the better. So, build a legacy of hope, determination, and growth. Build an empire of people who care for the greater good.

Tap into Your Inner Power: Your strength is endless and accessible to you anytime. Believe in yourself to tap into it! If that is challenging based on what life dealt you, start with small steps. Recount past successes to drown out doubts and setbacks. Be your first cheerleader. Live intentionally to move beyond surviving. When you embrace a life of purpose, you will have much control over your life's agenda.

<u>Seek Genuine Encouragement:</u> Would you agree forgetting how far you have come in tough times is easy? This is where genuine encouragement comes into play. It transcends empty praises and keeps you grounded. It gives hope, fueling the drive, to keep going despite adversities. Wouldn't life be easier if you could smell insincere praise before getting too close? Seek genuine encouragement. It keeps at bay those preying on your vulnerability.

Remember, no matter how difficult the next step is, you can build ladders to climb out of survival into intentional living. This journey could be lonely, but in the end, it pays off. You are still the most important person to yourself and the few in your world. So, as a gift to yourself, take care of yourself.

Let us delve into more: Practical Food for Thought.

Practical Food for Thought

Life can be unpredictable and throw unexpected challenges at you, leaving you feeling overwhelmed and needing a breakthrough. The practical tools in this guide can help you bridge the gap between where you are now and where you want to be. These tips are not just random advice but are nourishing food for your mind, packed with insights and actionable steps to support you regardless of your circumstances. Think of them as your ally on your self-care journey and expect remarkable results if you apply them. Remember, taking care of yourself is essential, and there is nothing to lose by doing so. As the gatekeeper of your growth, take steps toward your best self. Therefore, do not delegate your self-care role to someone else. Instead, take actions that guide your growth. Reflect on the commitment you are about to make for yourself.

Do you have what I call 'non-negotiable values?' These are principles or beliefs you hold dear to your heart. They guide your decision-making, actions, and behaviors. They nurture your best version, and there is no compromising.

Take deliberate steps toward becoming the best version of yourself, and that by itself is a journey, so you have to stay committed to self-care. So, strive to better understand who you are in every situation.

Consider every decision you make and every action you take as a brushstroke on the canvas of your life.

Then, ask yourself: "Am I taking care of the masterpiece that I am?" Your answers should be 'Yes' or 'I am still trying.'

As you travel onto this self-assessment path, let each answer and lessons learned guide you through life's complexities and be aware of your strengths and limitations. Use them as a compass, pointing you toward your most genuine self. You will know you are on the right path when the divergence between your 'wants' and 'needs' becomes apparent. The 'wants' yields temporary gratifications and can cost more than you can afford. If it cost sleepless nights and bending backward, it is too expensive. The 'needs' prioritize what matters and are sustainable. However, we know life is not a straight path and is full of unwanted surprises. Push forward and be ready to recalibrate your priorities. The goal is to find peace, happiness, and harmony from within as you cultivate a better relationship with yourself. So, make meaningful decisions.

Take care of yourself, maintaining good mental and emotional health. Process your thoughts and feelings. They are fundamental to your life balance. Understand how they influence your actions and decisions. It will give you an edge on life battles. As you ride your life rollercoaster, practice self-compassion. It is a secret weapon to ensure you reserve a plate of goodness for yourself with no apology as you serve others. Walk with your head held high, ready to shock yourself and whoever else trying to hold you down.

"This book may close, but please remember that your life's journey is more than another item on your to-do list. It is a sacred commitment to becoming the best version of yourself. Can I count on you to honor this responsibility, starting with taking care of yourself?"

Now, pick yourself up and charge forward, shattered masterpiece. Your great harvest awaits!

Summary

1. Seize the practical tools here to bridge the gap between where you are and where you want to be.
2. Reflect on your values and aspirations, aligning them with your growth journey.
3. Take deliberate steps towards your best self.
4. Shape your transformation with every decision and action.
5. Stay true to yourself, allowing the lessons from Mira's life and this guide to be your allies as you journey through challenges.
6. Prioritize needs over wants for meaningful decisions.
7. Practice self-compassion and nurture your well-being.
8. Take care of yourself, recharge, and process thoughts and feelings in ways that build you up.

No one understands how crashing is the burden you carry. So do not let anyone make you feel small. Look at Mira. She spent years searching for comfort outwardly. It took Mira coming home to Mira and understanding her worth to set sustainable emotional boundaries. In the end, she still helped and loved, but not at the cost of her sound mind. She learned to serve herself the same grace she shared with others.

Please, do not trade your life. It is yours to live and it is priceless. So, take care!

ACKNOWLEDGEMENT

Thank you to God, the Father, the Son, and the Holy Spirit. With the support of the Trinity, my life gained meaning, and I transcended from being a voiceless woman to echoing the timeless importance of self-love and self-acceptance. Jesus Christ's redeeming blood and the shepherding of the Holy Spirit rescued me from circumstances that tried to erase me. Publishing this book attests to how God breathed in my lifeless shell.

To my parents, as trailblazers, their worldview and wisdom made me a fearless woman. To my child, the one who stole my heart! Motherhood taught me unconditional love, which deepens unobstructed and puts my conscience on autopilot. When my best falls short, I find the strength to dig deeper. Also, a special thank you goes to my daughter, who, at 13 years old, created the art used for the book cover and, at 17, inspired the idea for the book.

To my family! There is no me without them. I thank God, who knows the purpose of familial bonds and that being born through our parents is not a foolish decision on His part. Through this lens of shared responsibility, I rise above life barriers, valuing family with greater depth. It is a critical path in my decision-making.

My brother-in-law, who read the countless iterations of this book, provided a second set of eyes that kept me focused.

To Pastor Saul and his wife, Mrs. Onilda. Their welcoming embrace showed me a nonjudgmental facet of leadership and mentorship.

To those whose paths intertwined with mine, you molded who I am. Together, we have navigated joyful and sorrowful rivers, deepening my appreciation for life and the wisdom of growing. You reminded me that as a product of God's mercy and grace, life is simple when lived through hope and love.

Dear readers, It is an honor you are reading this book. If you are a soul with untold stories and unsung melodies, remember to be truthful and kind to yourself. It will give you an edge in your battles. Take care of yourself with confidence, and there is no need to explain yourself. What God has given you is YOURS! Just do not carry unnecessary baggage; it will slow you down.

Hadassah,

Educator, Strategist, and Student of Life

"Thank you to all who walked or will walk in the fire to pull me out!"

I love you too!

ABOUT THE AUTHOR

Hadassah Mulowa K. Kajoba is a mother, Transportation Engineer, Psychologist, Philanthropist, and Consultant. After serving in the private sector, she now works as a Team Leader and Project/Contract manager in the public sector.

She founded the 'Galaxy of Universal Potentials (GO-UP),' a registered 501(c)(3) nonprofit organization promoting education and environmental stewardship to serve the greater good. With the support of many, she built a primary school in her native country, the Democratic Republic of Congo (DRC) in Africa. Over the past seven years, it has served hundreds of children in villages, yearly. In 2022, she founded the Life Simple Coaching & Consulting firm, offering creative approaches to addressing individual and organizational needs. The firm is based in America, where she also lives.

'**Shattered Masterpiece *The End Matters Finish Strong*'** *has made* Hadassah a debutant writer. As a storyteller, her messages are simple, practical, relatable, and they prioritize healing from within. Her blog offers life simple insights, which anyone can use as a companion through their life journey and in facing inevitable life adversities.

Hadassah is a Christ follower and a student of life. One of her most inspiring achievements is motherhood. She lives by a simple principle inherited from her late parents: "Fear no one but God. Everyone else deserves respect only." Learn more about Hadassah at www.TLSCC.com or contact her at Renewal@TheLifeSimple.Coach.

"When you serve goodness to others, don't leave your plate empty!"

Hadassah/Mulowa

www.ingramcontent.com/pod-product-compliance
Lightning Source LLC
Chambersburg PA
CBHW062224080426
42734CB00010B/2013